The Way, The Truth and The Life

Pupil's Book 4

Authors
Sr. Marcellina Cooney CP, Angela Edwards & Amette Ley

Editorial Team
Jennifer Clark, Kerry Malone, Joanne Ruff,
Frankie Strinati & Kate Welcome

Teachers' Enterprise in Religious Education Co. Ltd

Introduction

Welcome to *The Way, the Truth and the Life* series.

It is Jesus who said, "I am the Way, the Truth and the Life" (Jn. 14:6). These are very important words, so I would like each one of you to ask Jesus to help you to understand them.

In your lessons in Religious Education this year you will become familiar with the Bible: the story of God's love and concern for all of us. You will study Abraham, Joseph, Moses and David in the Old Testament.

In the New Testament, you will study the life of Jesus and some of his important teachings. You will also learn that Jesus is our Saviour and reflect on the meaning of his passion, death and resurrection.

As you progress through this book, you will come to know about the life of some of the early Christians; how the Church began and what it means to belong to it.

I hope you will enjoy your study and that each day you will grow closer to Jesus himself, who loves us and sends us his peace.

✠ Vincent Nichols
Archbishop of Westminster

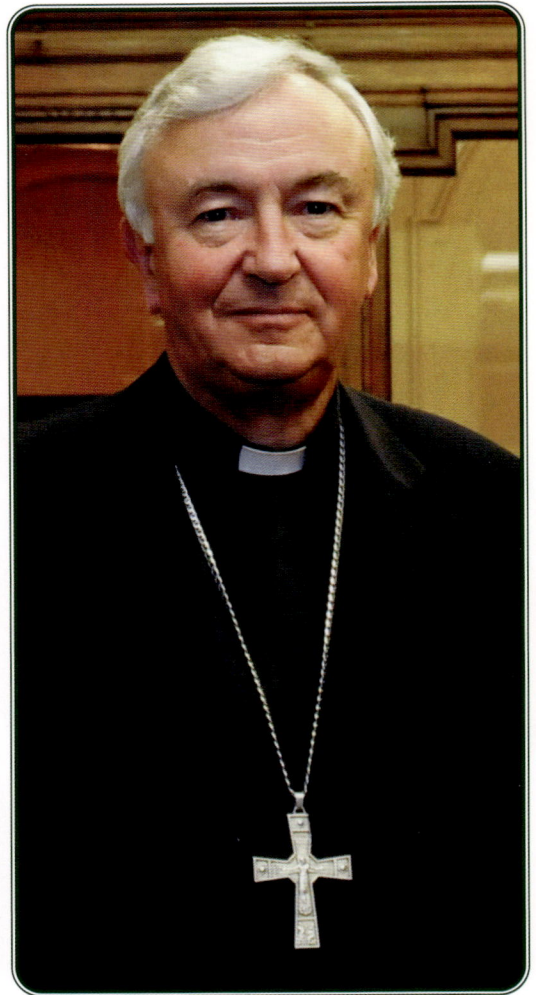

Contents

1. The Bible

What is the Bible?

The Bible is an account of God's relationship with His people, His concern for them and their response to His love.

The Bible was written over hundreds of years by many different writers. It begins with God creating the world and it goes on to cover the history of many people.

Each book in the Bible tells a part of the account of how God guides His people into the way of goodness, truth and love. Often people do not understand what God is telling them and some deliberately choose to go their own way. Others worship false gods, or fame and possessions.

No matter how many leaders, kings and prophets God sent, the people were not able or willing to live as God wanted; so He gave us the one person who could save us from sin and death. This was God's own Son, Jesus. He sent His Son into the world to save all people and that includes us.

1. a) Make a list of the stories from the Bible you already know.
   b) Which is your favourite one? Why?
   c) How does this story help you?
   d) How might it help other people?

2. Write a book blurb to give others an idea of what the Bible is about. Explain why it is important.

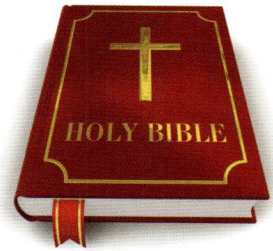

Books in the Bible

The first books of the Bible record the history of God's relationship with His chosen people, the Israelites. This section is called the Old Testament. The events in the Old Testament took place **before the birth of Jesus**, but they **point forward to his coming**. The Old Testament begins with the book of Genesis and usually ends with the book of Malachi.

The New Testament is made up of books about Jesus and the early Church. It begins with the Gospel of Matthew and ends with the book of Revelation.

The first four books in the New Testament are the Gospels of Matthew, Mark, Luke and John. These explain where Jesus was born, how he lived and died to save us and how God raised him to life again.

Some of the other books in the New Testament tell us about Jesus' followers, the early Christians. They explain how they set out to tell everyone they met about Jesus and how the Church began. The books of the Old and New Testaments were put together by the early Church to form the Bible.

a) What are the two main sections in the Bible?
b) What is the Old Testament about?
c) What is the New Testament about?
d) Why are they called Old and New Testaments?

How to use the Bible

Each book in the Bible has a name, for example, 'Matthew' is the name of the first book in the New Testament. This is short for its full name: 'The Gospel according to St. Matthew'.

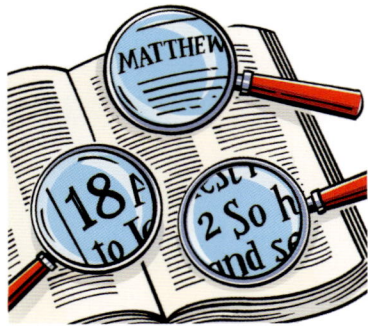

To make it easier to find your way around the Bible, each book is divided into **chapters** and each chapter is divided into **verses**. All the chapters and verses have their own number; (the verse numbers are very small) and the book names, chapter and verse numbers are written in a way everyone can follow.

Try looking up this reference: **Matt. 18:2-3.**

'Matt.' (short for Matthew) tells you which book to look in. You will find Matthew's Gospel at the start of the New Testament. Many Bibles will have all the books listed on the Contents page.

The first number, **'18'**, tells you which chapter of the book to look at. The numbers after the colon (:) **'2-3'** tell you which verse or verses from that chapter. So we have the Gospel of St. Matthew, chapter eighteen, verses two to three. Did you find it?

"So he called a little child to him and set the child in front of them. Then he said, 'I tell you solemnly, unless you change and become like little children you will never enter the kingdom of heaven'" Matt. 18:2-3.

Activities

1. Look at the Bible. What are the names of the first three books in the Old Testament and in the New Testament?

2. In the Old Testament God made many promises to His people.
   a) Find one or two of the references below.
   b) Write out the promise and put the reference next to it.

   Genesis 9:15   Isaiah 54:10   Isaiah 56:1

3. a) Look up the following Bible references:

   Luke 16:10   Mark 9:37   John 14:1

   b) Write down what each person said.
   c) Choose one of these references and say when it might help someone.

4. Would you find the following events in the Old Testament or in the New Testament?
   a) God created heaven and earth.
   b) The story of Noah, the flood and the ark.
   c) The angel Gabriel visits Mary.
   d) The baby Moses is left among the bulrushes.
   e) God speaks to Abraham.
   f) Jesus cures the blind man.
   g) Daniel in the lions' den.

5. Work in pairs or small groups.
   a) Choose one of the events from Activity 4 that you know about.
   b) Mime the story so that the rest of the class have to guess which one it is.

God's Plan for all People

We are now going to learn how God makes Himself known and how He begins to build a relationship of faith and friendship with us. This is not just a story of something which happened long ago; it is still happening.

We begin with the account of how God called Abraham and then learn about other famous people: Joseph, Moses and David.

God calls Abraham

God's Plan

Through Abraham, God shows His people that, if they have great faith and complete trust in Him, He will look after them.

God had a great love and concern for all people. However, for years many people turned away from Him, so He had to find people who were honest and who firmly believed in Him. He chose an old man, Abram, and told him to leave his own country and go to a land that He would show him. Abram said yes to God, even though that meant leaving his house and land. He packed up his belongings and set off with his wife, Sarah, not knowing where he was going.

God's Promise

Some time later, God made a promise to Abram and Sarah. He said the number of their descendants would be even greater than the stars in the sky or the grains of sand on the sea shore. He told him his name would not be Abram any more, but Abraham, which means 'the father of many nations'.

What great faith Abraham and Sarah must have had to believe all this, especially as they were both very old. Sarah was certainly too old to have babies. However, God always keeps His promises so after many years, the promise came true.

1. Role-play the conversation between Abraham and Sarah when he told her what God had asked him to do.
   - Think about all the difficulties of leaving home.
   - How would Abraham convince Sarah it was God who spoke to him?

2. a) Think of refugees who have to leave their home and country.
   b) How do they compare with Abraham and Sarah?
   c) What can we do to help refugees?

God Keeps His Promise

One very hot day, Abraham was sitting in the doorway of his tent, trying to keep cool. Perhaps he was dozing in the heat. Suddenly, he looked up and saw three men standing near him. Jumping to his feet, he bowed to them and asked them to sit down in the shade of a tree. It was very important in that hot country to make visitors welcome.

Abraham brought water to drink and more water so the men could wash their feet. While they rested in the shade, he ran into the tent and said to Sarah his wife, "Hurry! We have visitors; make some bread. While you do that, I will have some meat cooked". Then he hurried out to tell his servant what to do.

When everything was ready, Abraham brought the meat and bread with some butter and milk and gave it to his visitors. When they had finished eating, they said to Abraham,

"Where is Sarah your wife?"
"She's in the tent," answered Abraham.
Then the visitors told Abraham some amazing news.

"This time next year, we shall come this way again and Sarah will have a baby son."

Sarah was in the tent, listening to all this. When she heard about the baby, she laughed quietly to herself. "A baby", she thought – "I'm far too old to have babies".

The visitors heard Sarah laughing. "Nothing is too hard for God," they said and Sarah was sorry she had laughed.

Even though Sarah and Abraham found it very hard to believe that they would have a baby in their old age, they put their trust in God. Did you know that they had a son and called him Isaac, a name which means 'laughter'? (Gen. 21:1-6)

Activities

1. What does the story of Abraham tell us about:
   a) God?   b) Abraham?   c) Sarah?

2. Write an email to one of your grandparents to tell him or her what you have been learning about Abraham. Mention:
   • the difficulties he experienced;
   • the blessings he received.

3. In small groups, plan a TV programme about Abraham.
   • Think of a title that will make everyone want to see it.
   • Who will you include in it?
   • What events will you cover?
   • How will you convince the audience that it is a true account?
   • What is the most important thing that you will want the audience to learn from it?

Joseph

Know about God's call to Joseph.
Reflect on God's plan for him.

Joseph

When Isaac grew up, he had a son called Jacob. One day, God appeared to Jacob and told him that he would be the father to a nation. When Jacob grew up, he got married and had twelve sons.

Although Jacob loved all his sons, his favourite was Joseph. He gave Joseph a special coat with many colours to show how he felt. This made Joseph's brothers jealous. Worse still, Joseph had dreams about how his brothers would one day bow down to him. He told his brothers about the dreams. This made them very angry.

Activity

a) Was it fair that Jacob had a favourite son?   Give reasons.
b) Why were Joseph's brothers angry with him?
c) Were they right to feel like that? Why? Why not?

Dreams are shattered!

Joseph must have thought he was going to have a wonderful life. He had everything. He was his father's favourite son and he had an amazing coat to prove it. His dreams told him he was the most important of his brothers. What could go wrong?

He soon found out. One day, his father sent him out to the fields to see how his brothers were looking after the sheep. But, before he arrived, his brothers saw him coming. "Here comes the dreamer", they said. "Let's kill him and throw him into a pit and say a wild animal attacked him. Then we shall see if his dreams help him". Reuben, one of the older brothers, knew this was wrong. He tried to think what to do. "We won't kill him," he said. "We can just take his coat away and throw him into an empty well."

So that is what they did. After a while, some traders came along on their way to Egypt. The brothers sold Joseph to them as a slave. They took his coat and put an animal's blood on it. Then they told their father Jacob that Joseph was dead.

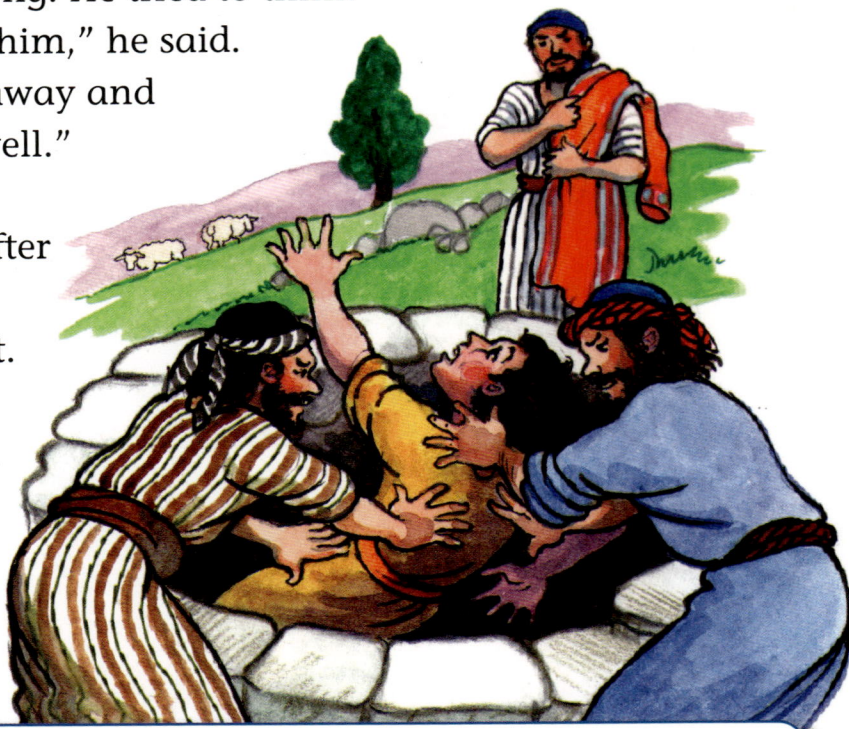

Activity

a) What did Joseph's brothers want to do with him?
b) Why do you think Reuben thought it was wrong?
c) God was looking after Joseph, but it was not very obvious. Why not?

Joseph in Prison

Joseph found himself in Egypt, working as a slave to a man called Potiphar. Potiphar was a kind master and Joseph worked hard, though he hadn't planned to be anybody's slave. However, Potiphar's wife didn't treat Joseph so well. She told such lies about him that, in the end, Potiphar believed her and sent Joseph to prison.

God is always with us when things are difficult. So, even in prison, God was with Joseph.

There were other people in prison with Joseph and they had dreams which they didn't understand. Joseph helped them to see what their dreams meant.

Activity

a) Use your Bible to read Gen. 40:9-19.
b) What interpretations did Joseph give to the prisoners' dreams?
c) How do you think the prisoners felt?

Pharaoh's Dream

Soon Pharaoh, the king of Egypt, heard about Joseph interpreting dreams. It happened that he too had dreams he didn't understand, so he called for Joseph to explain them. Joseph was glad to be able to help. He told Pharaoh that, for seven years, a lot of food would be grown in Egypt, more than people would need. After that though, there would be seven years where hardly anything would grow – a famine. Pharaoh would have to see that enough food was saved from the good years to feed the people of Egypt in the bad years. Pharaoh was glad to know about this. He immediately put Joseph in charge of organising the food storage. Joseph became a very important person.

Activity

a) Use your Bible to read Gen. 41:1-7.
b) What were Pharaoh's dreams?
c) In what ways was God helping Joseph?

Jacob's Problem

Jacob, Joseph's father, was very upset when he was told that his favourite son was dead. Now he had reason to be worried and upset again. There had been seven good years in his country too, but nobody there knew about the famine to come, so no food had been saved. When the bad years came, Jacob and his family were starving.

The land of Egypt, however, had plenty of food because of Joseph's plans. People came from all around to buy corn there. Joseph's father heard about all the food in Egypt and he sent his sons to buy corn too. Joseph was in charge of the food. The brothers came and bowed down to him. They didn't recognise him at first but Joseph told his brothers who he was. He gave them all the food they needed and told them to go home and bring the family back to Egypt. They could live there and have plenty to eat.

What a surprise his father must have had when his sons returned home. God had brought good out of evil and joy out of sadness.

Activities

1. a) Read Gen. 42:7. What is the connection between Joseph's first dream and what has now happened?
   b) Why do you think the brothers did not recognise Joseph at first?

2. What do you think the brothers told their father when they went back home? Think about:
   • what they first told him and why;
   • what questions their father asked;
   • the answers they gave; (Remember they will have to tell him what they did to Joseph many years ago).
   • what their father said to them when he knew the full story.

3. Frequently God uses people to help us.
   • Who were the people who helped Joseph?
   • What did they do?

God calls Moses

Know about God's call to Moses.
Reflect on what we can learn from his experience.

Life in Egypt

After Joseph had helped his brothers, they came to live in Egypt with their father Jacob. They were known as the Hebrews.

When Joseph's brothers married they had children and then their children had children. After the death of Joseph there was a new Pharaoh, the king of Egypt. He was worried that, because there were so many Hebrews in Egypt, they might cause trouble. So he treated them all like slaves, very cruelly. Also, he ordered that all the baby Hebrew boys were to be killed by drowning them in the river Nile.

One mother hid her son in a reed basket by the river Nile. Not long after, he was found and rescued by Pharaoh's daughter. She brought him up as her adopted son and gave him the name Moses.

Use your Bible. Read Ex. 2:1-10.

The Burning Bush

When Moses grew up, he left Egypt and lived in the land of Midian. One day, Moses was looking after sheep in the wilderness when he saw an amazing sight. A bush was on fire, blazing with flames, but instead of being destroyed, it kept burning. Moses went over to have a look. He couldn't understand why the bush was not destroyed.

As he came nearer, he heard a voice.

"Do not come any closer, Moses. Take off your shoes; you are standing on holy ground" (Ex. 3:1-6).
God was talking to him.

God gives Moses a Mission

God had much more to say to Moses. He reminded him that He was the God of Abraham, Isaac and Jacob. He could see how His people were suffering as slaves in Egypt and He had a mission for Moses.

"Go to Pharaoh, the king of Egypt and tell him to let my people go!"

Moses instantly panicked and said, "Who am I to go to Pharaoh and bring the sons of Israel out of Egypt?" God answered, **"I shall be with you"** (Ex. 3:10-12).

Moses produced all kinds of reasons why he couldn't do this. "Pharaoh won't listen to me," he said, "and even if he does, the Hebrews won't believe that you have spoken to me. Who shall I say you are?"

God said to Moses, "Tell them **'I AM who I AM'**".

Moses tried one last time. "I am really not very good at speaking," he said.

So God told Moses he could take his brother Aaron with him, as Aaron was good at speaking. Finally, Moses understood that he would have to try to persuade Pharaoh, no matter how impossible that seemed, but at least now he wasn't alone. He had his brother to help and God would be with him (Ex. 4:10-15).

⏸ Pause to reflect

The big promise that God made to Moses was: "I will be with you".

It means:
- Do not be afraid!
- I will be guiding you.
- I will be helping you.

Moses returns to Egypt

Moses went back to Egypt to tell the people, God's chosen people, that God had heard their prayers. God had spoken to him so he had come to help them. (It was around this time that the Hebrews became known as the Israelites).

Activities

1. a) What did God ask Moses to do?
   b) Would it be easy? Give reasons.
   c) What promise did God make to Moses?

2. Work in pairs, one of you is Moses. You go home and tell your wife what happened.
   a) Role-play the conversation. Think about:
      - what God has asked you to do;
      - how you feel about it;
      - the dangers and difficulties;
      - what your wife thinks you should do;
      - what God has promised you.
   b) You each write a diary entry about what happened.

3. Moses went to see Pharaoh, but he was not at all welcome. Imagine you are a TV reporter and have to investigate what happened. [Notes in TB pages 22-23]
   a) Describe briefly some of the events.
   b) Explain what happened to Pharaoh's son and why?

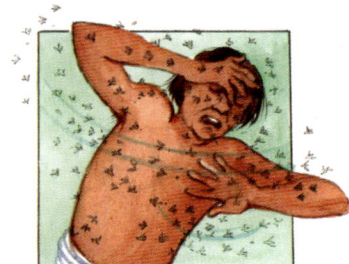

The Passover

The Israelites were told to get ready to leave. They had to cook and eat a special meal: roast lamb, bitter herbs and unleavened bread. They were to be ready for a quick getaway.

They had to mark the door frames of their houses with blood from the lamb. This sign meant the angel who was bringing the final plague would pass over the homes of the Israelites.

The Exodus

God heard the prayer of the Israelites. He guided and protected them as they left Egypt. But once they reached the banks of the Red Sea, they panicked. How were they going to get across?

Find out what happened.

Activities

1. a) Use your Bible. Read Exodus 14:21-29.
   b) What did the Egyptians do when the Israelites escaped?
   c) What did God tell Moses to do?
   d) What happened next?
   e) How do we know that God kept His promise to Moses?

2. Create a mime or a dance to show what the Israelites were feeling when they managed to escape.

3. In what way did God bring good out of evil and joy out of suffering for the Israelites?

David is chosen by God

Know that David was chosen by God.
Reflect on David's trust in God.

David is anointed King

Many years had passed since the time of Moses. God's people were settled in their own land and they had a king, Saul. Saul was not a good king so God sent the prophet Samuel to anoint the next king.
This was what God said to Samuel,

"Fill your horn with oil and go. I am sending you to Jesse of Bethlehem, for I have found myself a king from among his sons" (I Sam. 16:1).

Samuel did as God asked. He went to Jesse at Bethlehem and asked to see his sons. Jesse presented seven of his sons to Samuel, each of them tall and good looking, but each time God told Samuel, "This is not the one".

"Have you any more sons?" Samuel asked. Jesse told Samuel about the youngest, David, who was looking after the sheep.

"Send for him!" said Samuel.

When David came in, God told Samuel,

"Get up and anoint him – he is the one!"

So Samuel took his horn full of oil and poured it over David's head to anoint him as the new king of God's people. God's Spirit came down on David from that moment.

1. a) Why did Jesse not include David when Samuel asked to see his sons?

   b) Do you think Samuel anointed the right person? Give reasons.

2. God does not choose people by how they look or what they wear, but by what is in their heart. Draw a large heart. Put words in it to describe what you think God would like to find most of all in your heart.

3. Watch the Power Point presentation of David's brothers. What did they have to learn?

God helps David in battle

Although David had been anointed as the next king, he was still very young and Saul still ruled the Israelites. Sometimes Saul felt really depressed. David was gifted at playing the harp, so Saul asked him to play to cheer him up. David and Saul became great friends.

At this time, the Israelites were at war with the Philistines. The Philistines had a huge man, almost a giant, on their side. His name was Goliath. Every day, he would come out and shout,

"Send a man to fight with me! If he wins, we will be your slaves, but if I win you will be our slaves".

None of the Israelites had the courage to fight with him – he was such a giant.

David's brothers were at the battlefield, and one day David was bringing them food when he heard Goliath's shout. He went straight to King Saul.

"I will fight the Philistine, Goliath," he said. Saul must have smiled.

"You are only a boy," he said, "and Goliath is a powerful warrior." David insisted saying he had fought off lions and bears when he had looked after sheep. He was sure, with God's help, he could fight Goliath. So Saul agreed and had some of his own armour brought for David. It was too big and he couldn't walk in it, so David took it off. Then he chose five smooth stones from the river and put them in his shepherd's bag. He took his sling and a stick and set off to meet Goliath.

Goliath roared with anger when he saw David.

"I will feed you to the birds!" he threatened.

David stayed calm. He told Goliath that he trusted in God. Then he took one of the stones from his bag, put it in the sling, whirled it around his head and hurled it. The stone hit Goliath in the middle of his forehead. He fell to the ground dead. The battle was won. God had used David's trust in Him to save His people. (Adapted from I Sam. 17).

This account of David and Goliath teaches us that, when we face difficulties in our lives, we can overcome them by placing our trust in God as David did.

1. Discuss. Why do you think David offered to fight the giant?

2. Imagine David is telling his grandchildren about what happened to him and Goliath.
   a) What would he want them to learn from this story?
   b) How might David's experience help people who have to face big difficulties?

God Speaks to Us

Know that God speaks to us in the Bible.
Reflect on some things God tells us.

God speaks to us in the Bible

Sometimes the readings in the Bible are great – they help us to understand things, they encourage us, they comfort us when we are afraid or sad.

At other times, they remind us to love others and that is not always easy. Some readings can challenge us – like 'love your enemies'!

"I am the Way, the Truth and the Life" (John 14:6).

"You are precious in my eyes" (Isaiah 43:4).

"Pray for those who treat you badly" (Luke 6:28).

"God is always ready to forgive" (Joel 2:13).

"The Lord is my shepherd, there is nothing I shall want" (Psalm 23).

"Love your enemies, do good to those who hate you..." (Luke 6:27).

1. Slowly and quietly read the quotations on page 22.
   Read them a second time and think carefully about each one.
   a) Which one makes you feel happy?
   b) Make a copy of this one, use colour to show the key words.
   c) Write down underneath it why it makes you happy.

2. Look at the Bible references again.
   Which one will help a person …
   a) who is worried about something?
   b) to forgive when he/she has been hurt?
   c) who feels lonely?
   d) who needs to trust in God?

3. Work in pairs.
   Use two quotations from page 22 and one of the following to
   make a prayer card for Class Prayer. Choose ones most likely to
   help pupils in your class.

   Jn. 14:1   **Jn. 14:14**   **Jn. 15:17**

4. Choose one of the following: Abraham, Joseph, Moses or David.
   Look back on his life.
   a) Describe his relationship with God.
   b) Did he always know what God wanted? How do you know?
   c) What were the greatest challenges in his life?
   d) What were the blessings?
   e) What advice would you give to young people about trusting
      in God?

2. Trust in God

Understand the importance of trusting in God.
Be aware that it is not always easy for us to trust.

Learning to Trust

Jason was worried. On Saturday morning, his swimming lessons would start again. Last term, swimming had filled him with fear. He was frightened of the water. 'Listen to your instructor,' mum said. 'You can trust him.' Jason took mum's advice. He listened to the swimming instructor, did exactly as he was told and trusted that the water would support him. Before long, he was able to swim.

Not long afterwards, Jason heard his teacher talk about trusting in God and he wondered if it was like learning to trust the water in the swimming pool.

Activity

a) Listen to the story of how Tom and Abigail learned to trust. (TB p.36)
b) Write a 'list' prayer asking God to help you trust in Him.
    For example:
    When I am …. help me to trust in You.

A lesson for Jonah

Do you remember how people in the Old Testament like Abraham, Moses and David had to trust in God? Well, there was another man, Jonah, who found it very difficult to do what God asked him.

This is what happened. The people of Nineveh, a big city, were selfish and greedy. God asked Jonah to go there to tell them to change their ways and think about others.

Jonah did not have the courage to do it so he ran away to hide. In the harbour he found a boat which was about to set sail and jumped on board. Before long, the wind began to blow and the rain poured down. The boat was tossed up and down by enormous waves. The sailors had never seen anything like it. They were helpless and afraid. "God must be angry with us", they said. Then Jonah spoke up: "It's my fault, I'm trying to run away from God." So the men threw him overboard into the sea.

Before long, Jonah was swallowed by a whale. He prayed to God and asked for His forgiveness. After three days and nights in the whale's belly, the whale spat Jonah out onto a beach.

Jonah was ready to obey God now. He went back to Nineveh; he didn't expect the people to listen to him or believe him, but they did. They announced that they would all fast from food and wear sackcloth to show how sorry they were for all they had done wrong. Even the king joined in and God, who loves all people, forgave everybody.

It is important to remember that when the boat was tossed up and down by the enormous waves, God was teaching Jonah and all of us a lesson.

Activities

1. a) Why was it hard for Jonah to trust in God?
   b) What were the important lessons Jonah had to learn?

2. Discuss. Are there times in school when you don't want to do what God wants you to do?

3. Imagine you have the chance to talk to Jonah.
   a) What questions would you ask him?
   b) What do you think he would tell you?

TRUSTING - Important points to remember

God is all-powerful. He loves each one of us very much and sometimes, like a very good teacher, He challenges us so that our trust in Him will grow stronger. That means we may not always get what we want, because God knows what is best. We might have to wait a long time to know why God did not answer our prayer – but we will know some day.

Paula was very upset when her parents told her they were moving to England and would be leaving their home and friends in Brazil. She asked God not to allow this to happen. She could not speak a word of English so what was she going to do?

At first, it was very, very difficult for Paula. Now, she is delighted to be in a lovely school with lots of friends. She is able to speak English as well as Portuguese and can email her friends in Brazil.

Pause to share

Do you think God always answers our prayer?
Can you remember a time when you thought God did not answer your prayer? Think about what God's plan might be.

Activities

1. Choose somebody in the Old Testament who had to learn to trust in God. Briefly explain what happened.

2. Imagine your friend is very upset because his or her family is going to live in another country.
   Explain to your friend why it is important to trust in God.

3. Trusting in God.
   Draw a box. Use bullet points to put your own key points on trusting in God on to it.

Zechariah

God's promise to Zechariah

Sometimes things happen that take us completely by surprise. It can be really good news, sad news or strange news. It can be very difficult to see how some things can be part of God's plan for our lives.

For Zechariah, God's plan was unexpected news. Zechariah was a priest and one day he was in the Temple in Jerusalem burning incense and offering prayers to God. As he prayed, he looked up and saw an angel. It was the angel Gabriel.

Zechariah was afraid, but Gabriel had good news for him.

"Your prayers have been heard, Zechariah," he said. **"You and your wife Elizabeth are going to have a baby son. You must call him John. He will bring you great happiness. When he is grown up, he will help many people to love God. He will prepare a way for the Lord"** (Lk. 1:13-16).

Zechariah felt very happy to hear this, but wondered if it could be true. He and Elizabeth had wanted a baby for so long and now they were going to have a child who would be a great prophet. It was hard to believe such wonderful news.

"How do I know this is true?" Zechariah asked the angel.

The angel replied, "I am Gabriel who stands in God's presence. I have been sent to speak to you and bring you this good news. Listen! Since you have not believed my words, which will come true, you will be silenced and have no power of speech until this has happened" (Lk. 1:19-20).

Everyone in the temple was very surprised when they realized that Zechariah could not speak to them. Zechariah went home and waited.

1. Imagine you are Zechariah.
   Write down what he might have written for his family when he came home from the Temple.

2. Why do you think Zechariah didn't believe what the angel told him?

Birth of John

When the time came for Elizabeth and Zechariah's baby to be born, all their family and neighbours wanted to name him Zechariah after his father, because this was the custom.

"No," said Elizabeth firmly, **"his name is John."**

"But nobody in your family has that name," the people said. They gave Zechariah a writing tablet where he could write the baby's name.

Zechariah wrote, **'HIS NAME IS JOHN'.**

As soon as he had written this, he found he could speak again. God had kept His promise to Zechariah and all the neighbours wondered what John would grow up to be (Lk. 1:5-24 and 1:57-66).

Zechariah was filled with the Holy Spirit and was able to understand God's plan for all of us. He thanked and praised God. Then he told all the people present that the Saviour would come and bring God's loving-kindness to each one of us.

Later John became known as John the Baptist and he prepared the way for Jesus.

Activities

1. Think of all you know about Zechariah.
   a) What was God teaching him?
   b) Did he learn the lesson? How do you know?
   c) In what way did God's plan come true for Zechariah and Elizabeth?

2. Use your Bible to read Luke 1: 76-79.
   Explain what Zechariah foretold about his son John.

3. Zechariah was an important person.
   Use your ICT skills to write headlines for the local paper about some of the important things that happened to Zechariah and Elizabeth.

Mary trusts in God

The Annunciation

"In the sixth month, the angel Gabriel was sent by God to a town in Galilee to a young girl named Mary. He went in and said to her,

**'Hail Mary, full of grace!
The Lord is with you'.**

Mary was deeply disturbed by these words and asked herself what this greeting could mean, but the angel said to her,

**'Mary, do not be afraid;
you have won God's favour'"** (Lk. 1:26-31).

The angel explained to Mary that she would be the mother of a baby boy and she was to call him Jesus. He would be great and would be called the Son of God. Mary was puzzled because she was not married. She asked the angel how this would happen.

The angel told her that God alone would do it all.

30

"'The Holy Spirit will come upon you', the angel answered, 'and the power of the Most High will cover you with its shadow. And so the child will be holy and will be called Son of God'" (Lk. 1:35).

The angel Gabriel reminded Mary that nothing is too hard for God. Gabriel told Mary that her cousin Elizabeth, whom everyone thought was too old, was going to have a baby in three months time.

Mary let God take over in her life. God helped Mary to have absolute trust in Him. Mary said,

"I am the handmaid of the Lord; let it be done to me according to your word" (Lk. 1:38).

This was Mary's way of saying 'Yes, I trust you,' to God.

Mary had to wait. She trusted God to help her but she had no idea what He would do. However, she believed God always keeps His promises. Like Mary, we can learn to trust and have faith in God, because He loves us and wants us to be happy.

Activities

1. What can we learn from Mary's response to the angel?

2. a) Use your Bible. Look up the first words the angel spoke to Mary in Luke 1:28.
   b) Look up the words Elizabeth said to Mary in Luke 1:42.
   c) Which prayer do we say that uses words like these?

3. What thoughts might have come into Mary's head when the angel had left? Think about:
   • what she would tell Joseph;
   • what she might be most anxious about;
   • what she would be happy and excited about.

Joseph trusts in God

Know how Joseph put his trust in God.
Be aware that sometimes we need help to trust in God.

Joseph puts his trust in God

Mary completely trusted in God's plan for her to be the Mother of Jesus. She trusted God to look after her and teach her all she needed to know. Mary was engaged to a good and gentle man named Joseph. Now Mary had to trust God to help Joseph understand that her son would be the Son of God. God knew the right time and the right way to speak to Joseph about this.

The angel Gabriel came to Joseph in a dream and told him that Mary was to be the mother of Jesus and he was to be the foster father of Jesus.

The angel of the Lord said to him, **"Joseph, son of David, do not be afraid to take Mary as your wife, for that which is conceived in her is of the Holy Spirit: she will bear a Son and you shall call his name Jesus, for he will save his people from their sins"** (Matt 1:20-21).

Joseph always obeyed and trusted God. He married Mary and they lived in Nazareth. When Jesus was born, Joseph was a wonderful foster father.

Journey to Bethlehem

Mary and Joseph had been living happily in Nazareth for about six months when they heard that the Roman Emperor commanded everybody to go to the town their family had come from in order to be counted. This was because the government needed to know just how many people there were in the country.

Joseph's town was Bethlehem.

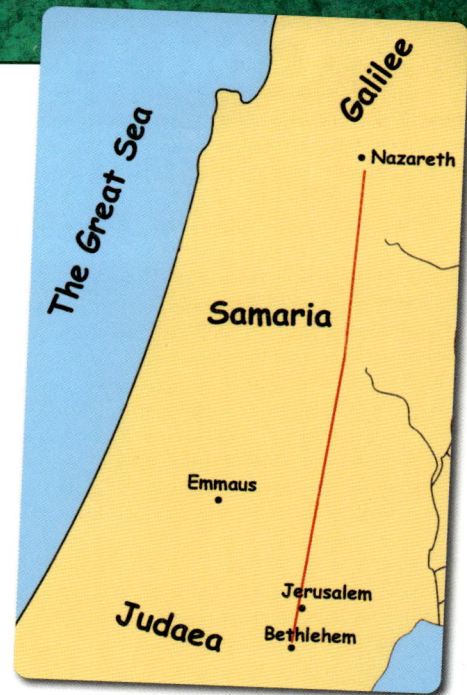

The Great Sea

Galilee

• Nazareth

Samaria

Emmaus
•

Jerusalem
•
Judaea   Bethlehem
•

Activities

1. There were no mobile phones or email so Mary and Joseph could not make an advance booking to stay in Bethlehem. What do you think they had to do?

2. Mary and Joseph did not know what was going to happen, but they knew about people in the Old Testament who had trusted in God.
   a) Who do you think they might have talked about?
   b) What might they have said?

3. How would you describe Joseph's character? Give reasons for your choice of words.

4. Work in pairs.
   a) Think of examples when we need to trust in God.
   b) When it might be easy?
   c) When it might be difficult?

God Fulfils His Promise

Know that God fulfilled His promise to Mary when Jesus was born. Reflect on the importance of the birth of Jesus for us.

The Birth of Jesus: God among us

When Mary and Joseph arrived in Bethlehem, every inn was full. Mary knew her baby would soon be born. Joseph was getting anxious and Mary was very tired so, they accepted the offer of a place in a stable with the animals. That night, Mary gave birth to Jesus.

She **"wrapped him in swaddling clothes and laid him in a manger, because there was no place for them in the inn"** (Lk. 2:7).

"In that region there were shepherds out in the field, keeping watch over their flocks by night. And the angel of the Lord appeared to them, and the glory of the Lord shone around them. They were filled with fear. Then, the angel said to them, **'Be not afraid; for I bring you news of great joy, a joy to be shared by the whole people. Today, in the town of David a Saviour has been born to you; he is Christ the Lord. And here is a sign for you: you will find a baby wrapped in swaddling clothes and lying in a manger"** (Lk. 2:8-12).

Activities

1. Use your Bible. Read Luke 2:15-20.
   • What did the shepherds do when the angel left?
   • Who did they find?
   • What did they tell Mary and Joseph?
   • What did Mary do?
   • Then what did the shepherds do?

2. Imagine you were one of the shepherds.
   Write an account of what happened to you.
   Explain why it was such an important experience.

The Wise Men

When Jesus was born in Bethlehem of Judea, Herod was the king. Some wise men from the East came to see him because they wanted to know where the new king had been born. They said, "We have seen his star in the east and we have come to worship him".

Fear gripped Herod. His mighty power was threatened. "A king? But I am the king", he must have said to himself. He called together all his chief priests and scribes to find out what they knew. They told him that the prophet Micah had said that a new ruler would be born in Bethlehem.

Herod said to the wise men, "Go and find out all about the child and when you have found him let me know, so I too can go to worship him" (Matt. 2:8).

The wise men followed the star which led them to the baby Jesus. They fell down on their knees and adored him. Then they offered him gifts of gold, frankincense and myrrh.

The wise men were warned in a dream not to go back to Herod, so they returned to their own country a different way.

Activities

1. a) What is puzzling about the visit of the wise men?
   b) What do you think they said to Mary and Joseph?
   c) Find out the meaning of the gifts they brought. (See Glossary)

2. Do you think Herod wanted to worship Jesus? Why? Why not? (Clue: Matt. 2:13).

Flight into Egypt

"When the wise men had departed, an angel of the Lord appeared to Joseph in a dream and said: 'Rise, take the child and his mother, and flee to Egypt, and remain there until I tell you; for Herod is about to search for the child, to destroy him'. And he rose and took the child and his mother by night, and departed to Egypt and remained there until the death of Herod. This was to fulfil what the Lord had spoken by the prophet, 'Out of Egypt have I called my son'" (Matt. 2:13-15).

Before Jesus was able to walk or talk, he was a refugee and had to flee to another country.

Activities

1. Imagine you are Mary or Joseph. Write to Elizabeth or Zechariah to tell them about the visit of the wise men and why you became refugees.

2. Make a grid for: Faith, Challenge, Blessings.
   FAITH: In what ways did Mary and Joseph have faith?
   CHALLENGE: What were the difficulties they faced?
   BLESSINGS: What did God do for Mary and Joseph?

Know why God sent Jesus to earth.
Reflect on who Jesus is for us.

Mystery of the Trinity

In order to understand why God came to earth, we must first think about the mystery of the Trinity – three persons in one God. This is a great mystery which God wants us to think about even though we cannot fully understand it.

Before the world was made, God was there as:

- Father
- Son
- Holy Spirit.

We call these **three persons in one God**, the **Holy Trinity**. The Father, Son and Holy Spirit were so filled with love that they wanted to share their love.

The Father created a beautiful world for us to enjoy and to look after.

The Son loved us so much that he came down to earth so that he could show us what God is like and so that we could share his life and love.

The Holy Spirit is the Spirit of God living in our hearts and guiding us to do the right thing.

The Trinity, or Three-in-One, has been made known to us by Jesus who was sent by the 'Father' out of love.

Mystery of the Incarnation

The mystery of the Incarnation means that God in Jesus became really human. He is truly and **fully God** and **fully human**. We believe this truth because God has told us.

So Jesus, who is truly God, was born as a little baby. Mary was his mother, so we call her Mother of God.

When we celebrate Christmas we are celebrating the birthday of Jesus, truly God, come down to earth to be with us and with all the people in the world. He came to save us from sin and death so that all who believe in him will have eternal life with him in heaven.

Activities

1. Work in pairs.
   Think of all the things you do in Advent to prepare for Christmas.
   Make a list. Highlight what you do:
   • to welcome Jesus in a special way;
   • to think of others.

2. When we look around the shops and the streets at Christmas, it is easy to forget what it really means for us.
   Design a poster to help people think about the real meaning of Christmas.

3. Imagine a friend asked you **why** Jesus came to earth.
   Explain in your own words what you would say.
   [For help see Pupil's Book 3 page 28 or the PPP on CD ROM]

4. a) What prayer do you know that reminds you of the Trinity?
   b) Write it out and decorate it.

3. Jesus, the Teacher

Know that Mary and Joseph took Jesus to the Temple.
Reflect on what this means for us.

The Presentation of Jesus in the Temple

Mary and Joseph were faithful Jews and when Jesus was just forty days old, they travelled to the Temple in Jerusalem to present him to God as the Jewish law stated:

"Every first-born male is to be dedicated to the Lord" (Lk. 2:23).

There was an old man named Simeon in the Temple. He was very close to God. God had made Simeon a promise that, before he died, he would see the Messiah, the Chosen One, sent by God to be a Saviour to His people.

Many people came and went every day in the great Temple but, when Mary and Joseph entered carrying their small baby, Simeon knew that they were special. This was what he had longed to see all his life.

Simeon took Jesus into his arms, blessed him and praised God for him. He knew that Jesus would grow up to be a **'light'** for all the people in the world. He was the long awaited Messiah. This is the prayer Simeon said,

"Lord, now let your servant depart in peace according to your word; for my eyes have seen your salvation which you have prepared in the sight of all the peoples, a light for the nations and the glory of your people Israel" (Lk. 2:29-32).

Simeon knew he had seen the Messiah. God had kept His promise.

Anna sees Jesus

Anna was a very elderly woman who stayed in the Temple day and night, praising God. She immediately knew that this baby was the child the Jewish people had been promised. Their long wait was over. Anna gave thanks to God for letting her see the Messiah. She told everyone she met that God had remembered His promise to them.

Every year, on February 2nd, we celebrate 'The Presentation of the Lord'. We remember Simeon thanking God for Jesus, the 'Light of the World'.

Activities

1. Why is the feast of the Presentation of the Lord important for us? Think about the words of Simeon.

2. Draw a large, lighted candle in the middle of your page. Write thoughts for Mary, Joseph, Anna and Simeon and put them around the candle. Write a title for your work.

3. Imagine you are Simeon. Write a letter or email to your friend, Nathan, describing your experience in the Temple.

4. Work with a partner. One is Mary, the other is Joseph. Imagine the conversation you have as you leave the Temple.
   Think about:
   - what Simeon said;
   - what Anna said;
   - how you plan to look after this little boy;
   - what you think his life will be like later on.
   Share with the class.

Jesus in the Temple

Know that Jesus was born a Jew.
Reflect on how Mary and Joseph found Jesus in the Temple.

Jesus was born a Jew

Jesus was born into a Jewish family. His parents, Mary and Joseph were faithful Jews and always followed the laws and practices of the Jewish religion. When they went to the synagogue in Nazareth on the Sabbath day, they took Jesus with them.

At the synagogue there are prayers and hymns. The people say together the **Shema** – a statement of what the Jewish people believe about God.

**"Listen, O Israel:
The Lord our God is one.
Love the Lord your God with all your heart and with all your soul
and with all your strength"** (Deut. 6:4-6).

Everyone listens while the word of God is read. After this, a rabbi or teacher, is asked to talk about the readings. At the end there is a blessing.

Activities

1. Use your Bible. Look up Deuteronomy 5:12.
   In your own words, explain what God asks the Jewish people to do on the Sabbath.

2. The Shema is a statement of what the Jewish people believe about God. Look up Deuteronomy 6:4-9.
   Write down what God asked His people to do to help them remember these words.

Mary and Joseph take Jesus to Jerusalem

Every year, Mary and Joseph used to go to Jerusalem for the feast of the Passover.

Activity

a) Use your Bible to read Luke 2:41-45.
b) Briefly describe what happened.
c) God had given Mary and Joseph His only Son - now he was missing! What do you think were their thoughts?

Three days later

Mary and Joseph found Jesus in the Temple, sitting among the teachers, listening to them and asking them questions. All who heard him were amazed at his understanding and his answers.

When his parents saw him they were astonished. His mother said to him, **"Son, why have you treated us so? Your father and I have been looking for you anxiously"**. He said to them, **"Why were you looking for me? 'Did you not know that I must be in my Father's house?"** But they did not understand what he meant (Lk. 2:46-50).

When Jesus replied to Mary and Joseph, he was thinking of his Father, God. Joseph was his foster father. Jesus went back to Nazareth and was obedient to them. He stayed there until he grew to be a man.

Activities

1. a) What question did Mary ask Jesus?
   b) Why did his reply puzzle them?
   c) What do you think he meant?

2. Mary and Joseph must have trusted God to keep Jesus safe until he was found. Write a prayer that Mary might have said while they were looking for Jesus.

The Baptism of Jesus

Know about the baptism of Jesus.
Reflect on what Jesus' baptism means for us.

Zechariah's Prophecy

When John the Baptist was born, his father Zechariah was filled with the Holy Spirit. He prophesied that Jesus, the Saviour would come and that John would prepare the way for him. Here are some of the things he said:

The Saviour will give light to those in darkness and guide us into the way of peace.

The Saviour is coming to save us from our sins.

The Saviour will make known the loving-kindness of the heart of our God.

At that time, many people had forgotten all the wonderful things God had done for them. They were not aware of their need for God and did nothing to help the poor people. So, before sending His Son, God chose John, who became known as John the Baptist, to prepare the way for Jesus.

Pause to discuss
- What do you think Zechariah means by people living in darkness?
- How do you think people can find God's peace?

Pause to reflect
- What does it feel like when you have done something wrong and you know you are completely forgiven?
- Remember Jesus loves us very much and will always love us.

John the Baptist

When John grew up he was a wild character! He lived in the wilderness and wore clothes made of camel hair with a leather belt around his waist and his food was locusts and wild honey.

Crowds flocked into the wilderness to hear John. He announced that the Messiah, the Saviour that they had been waiting for, was coming very soon. He warned the people that they needed to change their ways.
"Repent for the kingdom of God is at hand."
Then he quoted from the prophet Isaiah,

**"A voice cries in the wilderness:
Prepare the way of the Lord, make his paths straight" (Matt. 3:3).**

He warned them that God looks into peoples' hearts to see if they have faith and trust in Him. Also, He wants to see if they look after people in need of help.

Activities

1. The people wanted to know what they had to do to prepare for the Messiah. Use your **Bible** to find out two things John the Baptist said: Luke 3:10-14.

2. If you had been there, what questions would you have asked John?

3. Imagine John the Baptist coming today.
   - What would he look like?
   - How would he gather the crowds?
   - What do you think he would say?
   - How might you help and support him?

The Baptism of Jesus

The people of Jerusalem and all Judea and the whole Jordan district made their way to John to be baptised. Jesus appeared. He wanted to be baptised by John. But John said to him,

"It is I who need baptism from you and yet you come to me".

Jesus replied, **"Leave it like this for the time being."** By this Jesus meant that he wanted to live with the people and do what they did.

"As soon as Jesus was baptised, he came up immediately from the water, and suddenly the heavens were opened and he saw the Spirit of God descending like a dove and coming down on him. A voice spoke from heaven, 'This is my Son, the Beloved, my favour rests on him'" (Matt. 3:13-17).

Even John was taken by surprise. The **'heavens opened'** as though an invisible curtain was suddenly pulled back to reveal Jesus, the Son of God. The people could not believe their eyes.

The voice from heaven was God revealing to the people that Jesus is truly His Son, His only Son. The Father had sent His Son to be our Saviour.

The dove is a symbol of God's Spirit. It is also a symbol of peace. This is the peace that Jesus gives to all people who follow him and want to live a good life. So, when we open our hearts to God in prayer, He will give us His peace and show us how to live a good life.

Pause to discuss

When Jesus was baptised, the three persons of the Trinity were present. How do we know this?

The Public Life of Jesus

Following his baptism, "when Jesus was filled with the power of the Spirit he returned to Galilee. His reputation spread throughout the countryside. He taught in synagogues and everyone praised him" (Lk. 4:14-15).

Activities

1. How would you explain the baptism of Jesus to your family? You will need to include:
   • why John the Baptist did not want to baptise Jesus;
   • why Jesus wanted to be baptised;
   • what the voice said and what it meant.

2. Research. Use your **Bible** to read Luke 4:16-22.
   a) Explain in your own words what the prophet Isaiah said.
   b) What did Jesus say about this prophecy?
   c) What do you think he meant?
   d) What did the people think of him?

Disciples of Jesus

Know that Jesus called people to follow him.
Be aware that we are also called to follow Jesus.

Jesus chooses his first disciples

One day, "while the people pressed upon Jesus to hear the **word of God**, he was standing by the lake of Gennesaret. He saw two boats by the lake; but the fishermen had gone out of them and were washing their nets. Getting into one of the boats which was Simon's, he asked him to put out a little from the land. Jesus sat down and taught the people from the boat. When he had finished, he said to Simon,

"Put out into the deep and let down your nets for a catch".

Simon answered, **"Master we worked all night and caught nothing! But at your word I will let down the nets"** (Lk. 5:4-6).

When they had done this, they caught so many fish that their nets were breaking. They beckoned to their partners in the other boat to come and help them. They came and filled both boats so that they began to sink. But when Simon Peter saw it, he fell down at Jesus' knees, saying,

"'**Depart from me, for I am a sinful man, O Lord**'. For he was astonished, and all that were with him, at the catch of fish which they had taken. Jesus said to Simon, '**Do not be afraid; from now on you will be catching men**'. And when they had brought their boats to land, they left everything and followed him" (Lk. 5:1-11).

Activities

1. Simon Peter and Andrew heard the word of God from Jesus. Jesus asked them to do something. At first, they thought it would be a waste of time.
   a) What did they do? Why?
   b) What did they witness? Why?

2. When Simon Peter fell down at the knees of Jesus, he made a strange request.
   a) What did he say?
   b) Why do you think he said it?
   c) How do you think he felt when he heard Jesus' reply?

3. Discuss.
   a) Why do you think Simon Peter and Andrew were ready to leave everything, boats, nets and all, to be with Jesus? (Think deeply. Who do you think might have inspired them?)
   b) What would they gain and what would they lose by leaving everything to be with Jesus?
   c) Why might it be very difficult?

4. Use your Bible to read about the call of James and John.
   a) Read Mark 1:19-20.
   b) What did James and John do?
   c) How do you think their father felt when he saw them going with Jesus?
   d) What might he have said to them?

5. Work in groups.
   a) Think of all the ways we are called to follow Jesus.
   b) How might you encourage others to be followers of Jesus? You may use your ICT skills to present your work. Think about 'outward' and 'inward' commitment.

The Teaching of Jesus

Know that Jesus travelled around teaching people.
Think about the Good News that Jesus teaches.

Jesus' Mission

Jesus had been given a special mission. When he grew up, he spent a lot of his time teaching - he was a rabbi or teacher. He travelled around Galilee. Sometimes he taught in synagogues or outside on a mountain or beside a lake.

Huge crowds gathered to hear Jesus, sometimes as many as four or five thousand people! Everyone listened to his wonderful teaching about God's love for us.

Jesus taught the people that, if they believed in him and followed his teaching, they would live with him forever.

Pause to discuss
- Think of what it would be like to live in heaven forever with Jesus.
- "No eye has seen and no ear has heard the wonderful things God has prepared for all those who love Him" (1Cor. 2:9).
- What would you want heaven to be like?

Joys and challenges of following Jesus

Jesus never promised things would be easy if we choose to be one of his disciples. He explained that although we will have difficulties and problems many times in our lives, we can also find happiness and peace. By the way he lived, Jesus gave us an example of loving and helping each other. He knew that there is sin and hatred in the world, so he challenged this by living his life full of goodness and love.

"Love your enemies and pray for those who persecute you" (Matt 5:44).

"Love one another as I have loved you" (John 15:12).

Jesus explained that when we help others, we please him very much. He said that whatever we do to others, to people we don't know, even to people we think are not important, we do to him. He said that the time will come when he will say to people who help others,

"Come, you that are blessed by my Father! I was hungry and you fed me, thirsty and you gave me a drink; I was a stranger and you received me in your homes, naked and you clothed me; I was sick and you took care of me, in prison and you visited me" (Matt. 25:34-37).

The ones who truly followed Jesus will then answer him,

"When Lord, did we ever see you hungry and feed you, or thirsty and give you a drink? When did we ever see you a stranger and welcome you in our homes, naked and clothe you? When did we ever see you sick or in prison, and visit you?"

"Jesus will reply, **'I tell you, whenever you did this for one of the least important of these brothers of mine, you did it for me'**" (Matt. 25:37-40).

Activities

1. Why is it important that we follow the teaching of Jesus about helping others?

2. a) Make a list of six groups of people Jesus asks us to help.
   b) In pairs, choose one of these groups and suggest how you could help them.
   c) Present your ideas with illustrations to the rest of the class.

3. Our actions can spread outwards like ripples in a pool.
   Think of one small thing you could do to help someone, which could start a ripple effect. You may present your work as a diagram.

4. Find information on an organisation that helps one of these groups:
   • sick people;
   • refugees;
   • cold and homeless people;
   • elderly.

The Parables

Jesus used parables to teach people

Jesus often told stories when he was teaching people. We call these **parables**, that is, an earthly story with a heavenly meaning.

Why did Jesus use parables to teach people?

Jesus knew that the crowds enjoyed listening to stories especially those that were about things they recognized, like sheep and vineyards, money, possessions and sowing seeds.

He knew that people were more likely to remember things they were told in this way – stories are much easier to remember than teaching!

Jesus sometimes told stories that would make the people think. Often the story had something strange or unusual about it, which made them think even harder.

Frequently, Jesus told parables that not everyone understood. Even Jesus' disciples needed some of the parables explained to them.

The Parable of the Sower

1. a) Use your Bible. Read the Parable of the Sower (Lk. 8:4-8).
   b) What happened to the seeds? Put your answers in a table like the one below.

The soil where the seeds fell	What happened to them
On the path	
On the rocky places	
In with the thorns	
On good soil	

2. On the next page are the meanings Jesus gave to his disciples for the Parable of the Sower, but they are jumbled up.
   a) Read the meaning of the parable in your Bible (Lk. 8:9-15).
   b) Write down each description of where the seeds fell and its correct meaning.

(i) Those that fell by the path.

(iii) Those that fell among thorns.

(ii) Those that fell on rocky places.

(iv) Those that fell on good ground.

Meaning: Those that hear the message of God, understand it and live by it.

Meaning: Those that hear the message of God but forget or ignore it.

Meaning: Those who hear the message of God but give it up when trouble comes.

Meaning: Those who do not understand the message of God because the worries and pleasures of life have distracted them.

3. The Parable of the Sower has a meaning for us today.
   a) Think of things that would stop God's message taking root in our hearts.
   b) What might get in the way or distract us from living as Jesus asked us?
   c) What can we do to help God's message grow in our lives?

4. a) In groups of four, prepare a mime showing one of the different types of people in the Parable of the Sower.
   b) Take turns to present it to the rest of the class who will identify which kind of person you are.

The Parable of the Unforgiving Servant

Once there was a king who decided to sort out the money people owed him. When he began to work out who owed what, one of his servants was brought to him. This servant owed the king a large amount of money. He could not pay the king back, so the king gave orders that he was to be sold, with his wife and his children and all that he owned. Then the king would get his money back.

The servant was really upset. He knelt down before the king and said, "Please, just give me some time and I will pay you everything I owe".

The king felt very sorry for him, and said he would let him off the debt. He would not have to pay back any of the money.

The servant was very glad to hear this, and he left the room.

As he went out, he met one of his fellow servants who owed him a small amount of money.

"Pay me what you owe at once," he shouted, grabbing him by the throat. The other servant knelt down in front of him.

"Please, just give me some time and I will pay you everything I owe," he said.

But the first servant refused and had his fellow servant put in prison until he could pay.

When all the other servants saw what had happened, they were very sad. They went to the king and told him all about it.

The king was angry. He sent for the first servant again.

"You wicked servant!" he said. "I let you off all the money you owed me, just because you asked. You should have done the same for your fellow servant."

And the king had him sent to prison until he could pay everything he owed.
(Adapted from Matt. 18:23-35).

1. a) Use your Bible to read the 'Unforgiving Servant' (Matt. 18:23-35).
   b) Who do you think is most like God in this parable?
   c) What is the lesson for us in this parable?

2. Imagine you are going to make a DVD of the 'Unforgiving Servant' and what happened to him. Design a cover for your DVD. Write part of the story on the back so that people will want to find out more.

3. a) What do you think would have happened if the first servant had let the second servant off the money he owed?
   b) Write a different end to the Parable of the Unforgiving Servant.
   c) What would Jesus have said to the people at the end of your story?

4. Jesus usually told parables about things people knew about. If he was telling parables today, he might tell them differently. Tell the story of the 'Unforgiving Servant' as if it happened today. You could present it as a storyboard or a TV script.

5. Design a wall poster to illustrate your favourite parable. Make sure the main characters are bold and clear and that the message is obvious.
   Think about the Parable of:
   • The Lost Sheep
   • The Good Samaritan
   • The Sower
   • The Unforgiving Servant
   • or another parable you know.

4. Jesus, the Saviour

Know that Jesus is truly God and, as man, truly human. Reflect on what this means for us.

Jesus, truly human

When Jesus was born, he was a tiny baby just like all babies. He lived with Mary and Joseph in their house in Nazareth. He loved his family very much and Mary and Joseph took great care of him. They shared many happy times as a family and some sad times too.

He grew up and went to a Jewish school. He had to study and he played with the other pupils.

When Jesus got older, he liked having good friends like Martha, Mary and their brother Lazarus. When he heard that Lazarus had died, he wept. He liked celebrating with people and went to weddings. Many people thought he was a wonderful person. He made lots of friends, particularly among sinners, the poor, the sick and the beggars. He visited their homes and had meals with them.

Quick Quiz

Use your Bible to read Lk. 19:1-10.

- Who was the tax-collector that Jesus chose to visit?
- Was he a good man? Why? Why not?
- Were the people happy to see Jesus speaking to him?
- What happened after his meeting with Jesus?

Sayings of Jesus

People loved listening to Jesus and enjoyed being with him. However, at times, he really made them think.

"When you give alms don't let your right hand know what your left hand does" (Matt. 6:3).

Pause to discuss

What do you think Jesus meant?
Think of examples to explain the meaning.

Occasionally, Jesus made some people feel uncomfortable, particularly if they were rich and did not share with others, for example, he said,

"It is easier for a camel to pass through the eye of a needle than for a rich man to enter the kingdom of God" (Lk. 18:25).

Jesus was not condemning people with money. However, he was giving a direct message to those with money who did not help the poor, the homeless and those who were starving.

Another time, Jesus got really angry when he found people selling their goods in the Temple. He drove them out saying,

"My house will be a house of prayer. But you have turned it into a robbers' den" (Matt. 21:13).

Activities

1. Read again the text 'Jesus, truly human'.
   Make a list of all the examples to show Jesus was human.

2. Research. Use your Bible to find more examples to show Jesus was truly human. For example:

   Jn. 4:6   Lk. 2:51-52   Mk. 15:37

Jesus, truly God

As a man, Jesus is truly human, but he is also truly God. This happened at the Incarnation – God became human. This is a mystery which we accept in faith.

> **"God loved the world so much**
> **that He gave His only Son,**
> **so that everyone who believes in him may not be lost**
> **but may have eternal life"** (Jn. 3:16).

God sent his Son, Jesus, into the world to save us and give us eternal life. The disciples had difficulty understanding this but, when they saw Jesus work miracles, they knew he was no ordinary person.

They saw him cure the paralysed man. "Before their very eyes the man got up, picked up what he had been lying on and went home praising God" (Lk. 5:25).

Quick Quiz

Use your Bible to read Lk. 5:17-26.
- Was it easy for the friends to bring the paralysed man to Jesus? How do you know?
- What did Jesus admire about these men?

Jesus calms the storm at sea so that even the winds and the waves obey him (Mk. 4:35-40).

The disciples also saw Jesus cure the man born blind (Mk. 8:23-26).

Quick Quiz

Use your Bible to read Matt. 4:35-41.
What does this account tell us about Jesus
- being human?
- being God?

⏸ Pause to reflect

Can you think of other miracles Jesus worked?
Share what you know about them with the class.

Jesus not only did many extraordinary things, but he said many things to show that he was speaking the words of God.

Jesus is the 'Word of God'. He spoke with great authority: he told us we have to love our enemies, do good to those who hate us and pray for those who persecute us.

He showed us how to do this when he was dying on the cross. It is certainly not easy to love our enemies or to do good to those who hate us, but with Jesus' help it is possible.

Activities

1. Jesus is truly God but he is also truly human.
   a) Think of all the things you already know about him.
   b) Draw two boxes. Using bullet points, in one give reasons to show how you know Jesus is truly human and in the other that he is truly God.

> Jesus is truly human because …

> Jesus is truly God because …

Some more references to help you.

(Mk. 1:40-42)   (Mk. 3:1-6)   (Jn. 11:25)

2. We believe Jesus is truly God and, as a man, truly human. In order to remember this mystery about Jesus, copy and highlight it in your own book.

Holy Week

Jesus enters Jerusalem

Do you know what happens when famous people arrive in a town after some great achievement like winning the World Cup or a medal at the Olympics? Everybody greets them, flags are flying and there is great excitement.

Over two thousand years ago, the people of Jerusalem greeted Jesus in much the same way. Many people spread their coats or put palm branches along the road.

Most people waved and shouted, *"Hosanna! Blessings on him who comes in the name of the Lord!"*

Some people believed that Jesus had arrived in Jerusalem ready to declare himself their king. Others like some religious leaders were jealous of him. Political leaders believed he would be a threat to the nation.

Pause to discuss

- Look at the picture on page 62.
- Who do you think the people are who are looking very happy?
- Can you find the religious leaders?
- How do you think they are feeling?
- Are you able to spot the political leaders?
- What do you think they are saying to themselves?

What did Jesus know?

Many people greeted Jesus as their king, but Jesus knew that he was going to Jerusalem for a very different reason. He knew that the only way he could bring us very, very close to God was to suffer and to die. He wanted to offer his life for us.

Activities

1. a) Use three groups of 'thought bubbles' to show what:
   - the friends,
   - the religious leaders,
   - and the political leaders were thinking about Jesus.
   b) What do you think Jesus would have wanted to say to each of them?

2. Use your Bible to find out what happened on the Wednesday of Holy Week, Matt. 26:14-16. Write it in your book.

3. If Jesus entered your town, what sort of welcome would you organise? Think about:
   - What would you do to let the people know he was coming?
   - Who would you invite to greet him first? Why?
   - Who would you take to see him?

4. What do you think Jesus would want to say to the people if he came to your town? Give reasons.

Holy Thursday

Understand what happened on Holy Thursday.
Reflect on how we can show our love for Jesus.

The Last Supper

Every year, Jewish people share a special meal together called the Passover. Jesus told the apostles that he had been longing to eat this Passover meal with them before he suffered.

So when they were all settled around the table, **"Jesus took some bread, and when he had given thanks, broke it and gave it to them, saying, 'This is my body which is given for you. Do this in remembrance of me'. Taking the cup, Jesus said, 'This cup which is poured out for you is the new covenant in my blood'"** (Luke 22:19-20).

The Meaning of the Last Supper

The Last Supper which Jesus shared with his friends was a Passover meal. This meal was very important for all Jews because it was the time when they remembered how God had freed them from slavery in Egypt. God told Moses that every family had to sacrifice an unblemished (perfect) lamb. They were to put its blood on the doorpost so that the Lord would 'pass over' their house without striking dead the first born. At the first Passover, the blood of the lamb was a sign of life. This was the beginning of the Israelites' freedom from the Egyptians.

At the Last Supper, Jesus gives a new meaning to the Passover meal: he was offering **himself** as the perfect sacrifice to free us from the slavery of sin.

This was a perfect sacrifice because Jesus was the sinless, unblemished Lamb of God. He freely accepted this suffering. He offered his life in love to his Father. Through his suffering and death, Jesus opened the way to heaven for us.

Pause to discuss

Look carefully at the picture of the Last Supper.
- Who do you see leaving the room?
- What do you think is happening? (Clue Matt. 26:14-16).
- How do you think Jesus is feeling?

Activities

1. a) What happened at the first Passover? (Re-read page 18).
   b) Explain in your own words how Jesus gave a new meaning to the Passover.
2. Make a Holy Week diary and fill it in as you learn what happens. (Outline on CD ROM)

Day	What happened?	Scripture Reference
Passion (Palm) Sunday		Mark 11:1-11
Wednesday		Mark 14:10-11
Holy Thursday		Mark 14:17-25 Mark 14:32-47
Good Friday		Mark 14:66-72 Mark 15:1-39
Easter Sunday		Mark 16:1-8

Gethsemane

Jesus had invited his disciples to share his last hours with him. After they had finished their Passover meal, they went out of the city to the Garden of Gethsemane.

Jesus knew that he was going to suffer and to die. So he took with him the disciples who were his closest friends, Peter, James and John. He asked them to stay awake and watch and pray.

Jesus moved a little way off and began to pray. He asked his Father to save him from all the things that were going to happen.

However, Jesus knew that the most important thing was to do what his Father wanted him to do, so he said, **"Let it be as you, not I, would have it"** (Mk. 14:36).

After accepting what the Father had planned for him, Jesus went back to the disciples and found them sleeping. He woke Peter and said, **"Had you not the strength to keep awake one hour? You should be awake and praying not to be put to the test"**.

Jesus went away and prayed. When he went back to the disciples, they were sleeping again. He told them that they could take their rest. **"My betrayer is close at hand"**, he said.

Judas, one of the twelve disciples, led the guards to the Garden of Gethsemane and handed Jesus over to them.

Activity

a) Read the above passage again. Can you find three things which caused Jesus to suffer?
b) Which one do you think caused him to suffer most of all? Why?

Peter's denials

After Jesus had been arrested, Peter followed at a distance and watched as Jesus was taken to the house of the High Priest. While Jesus was taken inside, Peter remained outside in the courtyard warming himself at a fire with some others. As he waited there, a maid recognised him and called out, "You are a friend of the man called Jesus." But Peter denied it. "I don't know him," he said.

A little later, a man saw him and also recognised him, "You are one of those who follow Jesus". And again Peter denied it. "I am not," he said.

About an hour later, someone else called out, "You're one of the friends of the man who's been arrested". As Peter denied this yet again, he heard a cock crow and realised the night was ending. He remembered Jesus' words: "Peter, you will let me down three times before this night is ended".

Jesus was right. Peter had let him down, not once, but three times. Peter went out of the courtyard and wept bitterly (Lk. 22:54-62).

However, this was not the end of the story. Jesus had said that no matter how often people have hurt us, we must always be ready to forgive them. He loved Peter and he forgave him for letting him down badly three times.

Activity

Jesus was arrested even though he was innocent. One of his closest friends denied knowing him and the others ran away.
  a) Why do you think Peter was such a coward?
  b) What would you have done if you had been there?
  c) Why do you think Jesus forgave Peter?

Good Friday

The death of Jesus

Jesus must have felt very alone as Thursday night turned into Friday morning. All his friends ran away; they deserted him. Judas had betrayed him.

The Jewish leaders had decided that he was guilty because they were jealous of him. Also, they were afraid that Jesus would make himself king so they sent him to Pilate, the Roman Governor.

At Passover time, Pilate used to release a prisoner for the people, anyone they requested. Pilate asked them if they wanted him to release Jesus or Barabbas, a murderer.

The Jewish leaders had encouraged the crowds to ask for Barabbas. The crowds shouted for Jesus to be crucified. Pilate was anxious to please them so he handed over Jesus to be crucified.

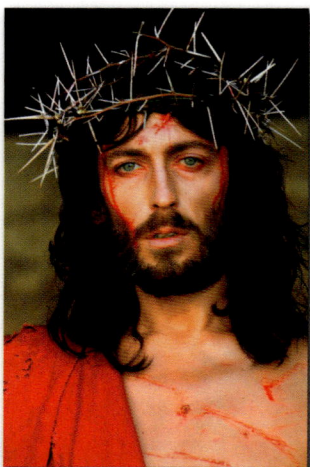

After this, the soldiers twisted some thorns into a crown and put it on his head.

Then they put a heavy wooden cross on his shoulders and led him to a place called Calvary or Golgotha where criminals were executed.

There the soldiers nailed Jesus to the cross and left him to die.

Jesus prayed for the people who had done this, asking his Father to forgive them.

On either side of him there were two thieves being executed. One called to Jesus and asked him to forgive him. Jesus replied that he would take him to paradise that same day.

In the last moments of his agony, Jesus offered himself to his Father and died.

His friends took his body down from the cross and carried it to a new tomb that had been carved out of the rocks. It was nearly evening, so they hurriedly wrapped his body in cloths.

They rolled a heavy stone in front of the tomb to make sure that no one would disturb it and went away.

Activities

1. a) Why did Pilate give in to what the crowds demanded?
   b) What is the lesson here for us?

2. Jesus did three things when he was dying on the cross.
   a) What were they? (Clue: Lk. 23:34; 43 and verse 46).
   b) What can everyone learn from his example?

3. Update your Holy Week diary.

Death on a Cross – WHY?

Begin to understand why Jesus died on a cross.
Think about what this means for us.

Why did Jesus die on a cross?

The reason why Jesus was crucified and died on a cross is a mystery which we cannot fully understand, but the Bible does help us.

Adam and Eve

We go back to the very beginning, to the time of the first human couple whom the Bible, in the Book of Genesis, calls Adam and Eve.

Adam and Eve were created in the image and likeness of God who is all good. At the same time, Adam and Eve were given the gift of freedom to choose to obey God or go against Him.

Freedom abused

Freedom is a very important gift because we can only truly love if we are free. Adam and Eve used their freedom to do evil rather than good. They disobeyed God. The first sin was committed which affected all future generations.

Activity

Adam and Eve used their freedom to choose to disobey God.
a) Make a list of all the opportunities you have today when you can freely choose to do something for others to show your love for Jesus.
b) Explain how your good choices could make a difference to the lives of others.
c) How do we know that when we help others, we are helping Jesus? (You will find the answer on pages 51-52).

Jesus offers His Life

Perfect friendship with God could be restored only by a perfect offering. So Jesus, who was without sin, offered himself to the Father for us. He was the perfect sacrifice.

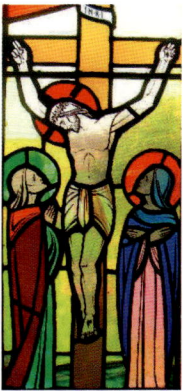

His death on the cross is the greatest sacrifice of love that anyone has ever made.

The Father accepted the sacrifice of His Son for our salvation because of His tremendous love for us. Jesus' loving sacrifice was so perfect, that it conquered death and he rose victoriously.

We call the Friday on which Jesus died **Good Friday** because on this day, Jesus made it possible for us to enjoy heaven forever.

Activities

1. a) What does 'salvation' mean? (For help, use the glossary)
   b) What did Jesus do for us by dying on the cross?

2. Explain why **Good Friday** is both a sad and a happy day.

3. Many people do not understand what happened on Good Friday and why Jesus died for us.
   Work in pairs to make a poster to explain what happened.
   Think about:
   • what pictures you will use;
   • how you will explain:
     ◦ what happened;
     ◦ why it happened.

4. We make little sacrifices when we **let go** of what we **want** in order to **help** others.
   a) Listen to the story of the two Japanese boys, Itsu and Takeo.
      (TB p. 67)
   b) Think of a little sacrifice you can make today to show your love for Jesus.

The Resurrection of Jesus

Understand what happened on Easter Sunday.
Reflect on the importance for us of the resurrection of Jesus.

Jesus appears to Mary of Magdala

Early on Sunday morning, Mary came to the tomb while it was still dark. She found the stone had been rolled away and Jesus' body was gone.

"Mary stayed outside near the tomb, weeping. Then, still weeping, she stooped to look inside, and saw two angels in white sitting where the body of Jesus had been, one at the head, the other at the feet. They said, **'Woman, why are you weeping?'** **'They have taken my Lord away'**, she replied, **'and I don't know where they have put him.'** As she said this she turned round and saw Jesus standing there, though she did not recognise him. Jesus said, **'Woman, why are you weeping? Who are you looking for?'**

Supposing him to be the gardener, she said, **'Sir, if you have taken him away, tell me where you have put him, and I will go and remove him'**. Jesus said, **'Mary!'** She knew him then and said to him in Hebrew, **'Rabbuni!'** which means Master.

So Mary of Magdala went and told the disciples that she had seen the Lord and that he had said these things to her" (Jn. 20:11-18).

The Resurrection of Jesus

What does it mean for us?

On the third day after his death, Jesus rose from the dead **body and soul**. The resurrection of Jesus is a real sign that death is not the end of our lives but a beginning of a new life in Jesus. It shows us how precious and valuable our lives are. Also, when this earthly life comes to an end, we can be sure that if we have trusted our lives to Jesus and followed his teaching, we will be with him in heaven for ever.

Activities

1. a) What do you think the Resurrection of Jesus meant for Mary of Magdala?
   b) What does it mean for you?

2. Complete your Holy Week diary.

3. Work in groups. Choose one of the following days. Write a newspaper article to explain its importance.
   • Passion (Palm) Sunday
   • Holy Thursday
   • Good Friday
   • Easter Sunday

4. Explain why the events of Easter Sunday make Easter the most important feast in the Church's year.
   Think about:
   • what happened;
   • what it means for us.

5. The Early Christians

Jesus appears to the disciples

After Jesus had risen from the dead, the disciples met him several times.

One night Peter said, "I am going fishing," and some of the other disciples said they would go with him. They got into the boat and fished all night long on the Sea of Galilee, but they didn't catch even one fish.

Just as the day was breaking, the disciples saw Jesus standing on the beach, but they did not recognise him. Jesus called to them,

"Have you any fish?"

"No," they called back.

"Put down the net on the right side of the boat," Jesus told them, "and then you will find some" (John 21:1-6).

Activity

Use your Bible to read John 21:1-13.

a) Did the disciples have a good night fishing?
b) What happened when they obeyed Jesus?
c) What did they see when they came ashore?
d) What did Jesus invite them to do?

Jesus makes Peter head of the Church

"After the meal, Jesus said to Simon Peter, **'Simon, son of John, do you love me more than these others do?'** He answered, 'Yes Lord, you know I love you'. Jesus said to him, **'Feed my lambs'.** A second time Jesus said to him, **'Simon son of John, do you love me?'** He replied, 'Yes, Lord, you know I love you'. Jesus said to him, **'Look after my sheep'.**

Then, Jesus said to him a third time, **'Simon son of John, do you love me?'** Peter was upset that he asked him the third time, 'Do you love me?' and said, 'Lord, you know everything; you know I love you'. Jesus said to him, **'Feed my sheep'"** (Jn. 21:15-17).

Perhaps Peter felt sorry, remembering the night when Jesus was arrested and taken to the High Priest's House. That night, Peter had denied three times that he even knew Jesus. But Jesus gave Peter three chances to put that right when he asked if he loved him. Peter knew he was forgiven. Jesus asked him to look after his Church. Peter had to get ready to be the first leader of the Church on earth, the first Pope. It was not going to be an easy task.

Activities

1. a) Why do you think Jesus trusted Peter again after he had let him down so badly?
   b) How do we know Jesus trusted him?
   c) How do you think Peter felt about this second chance?

2. Draw three thought bubbles. Fill them with thoughts that might have come into Peter's head during his conversation with Jesus.

3. Discuss.
   a) What do you think Jesus meant by asking Peter to feed his 'lambs and sheep'?
   b) How might Peter do this?
   c) What does this mean for us?

Pentecost

The Ascension

Jesus knew that he would soon be returning to his Father. He explained to his closest disciples that he would send his Spirit, the **Holy Spirit** to be with them.

He promised that the Holy Spirit would help them to remember and understand all that he had taught them.

Then he told them to go back to Jerusalem and to stay in the city until the Holy Spirit came to them. When that happened, Jesus said they would be his witnesses throughout the whole world.

When he had finished speaking, Jesus led them a little way out of the city. He lifted up his hands, blessed them and, while they watched, he was taken up and a cloud hid him from their sight.

The apostles returned to Jerusalem. They were joined by Mary the mother of Jesus, together with several women. They locked themselves in the upper room and they prayed continuously (Acts 1:12-14).

Activity

Study the faces of the apostles.
- How do you think they were feeling?
- Do you think they understood what the Holy Spirit would do?
- What questions do you think they asked Jesus?
- What questions would you have wanted to ask? Why?

Pentecost

About ten days later, the apostles with Mary were praying in the upper room when, "Suddenly they heard what sounded like a powerful wind from heaven, the noise of which filled the entire house. Something appeared to them that seemed like tongues of fire; these separated and came to rest on the head of each of them.

They were all filled with the **Holy Spirit**, and began to speak foreign languages as the Spirit gave them the gift of speech" (Acts 2: 1-4).

The Holy Spirit had come to them just as Jesus had promised. They were immediately filled with new strength and a power that would give them courage to speak publicly about Jesus. They praised God and thanked Him for this gift. These frightened fishermen became courageous apostles.

Crowds of people came running to see what was going on. Peter stood with the other apostles and spoke to the crowd in a loud voice.

> **Jesus is the Son of God.**
> **He died and rose again.**
> **He ascended into heaven.**
> **He has sent the Holy Spirit today.**

All the people were amazed. "What shall we do?" they asked Peter. This was the message that Peter gave them,

> **"Repent and be baptised so your sins will be forgiven.**
> **You will receive the gift of the Holy Spirit.**
> **This promise is for you and your children, and for all who are far away"**
> **Acts 2:39.**

That day, the apostles were freed from all fear and began to speak openly and with self-confidence. About three thousand people were baptised. This is how the Church was born. From the day of Pentecost, the Church has continued to spread the Good News all over the world to the end of the earth (Acts 1:8).

1. Work in groups. Using words and pictures design a storyboard to illustrate the coming of the Holy Spirit at Pentecost.
   Group 1 – Disciples huddle together in the upper room.
   Group 2 – The Holy Spirit comes down on the disciples.
   Group 3 – The disciples start speaking foreign languages.
   Group 4 – The disciples, full of new courage, greet the crowds.
   Group 5 – Peter gives the Good News to the crowds.
   Group 6 – Thousands of people are baptised.

2. Create a section of a dictionary to give the meaning of the following words. You may wish to use a computer.

   Disciple   **Apostle**   **Baptise**

   Pentecost   **Forgive**   **Sins**

3. a) Read St. Paul's letter to the Galatians 5:22-23.
   b) What does he tell us that the Spirit brings?
   c) Choose three of the fruits of the Holy Spirit.
      How can we make these fruits grow in us?

   Patience

   Love

   Gentleness

   Peace

   Self-control

   Faithfulness

   Kindness

   Joy   Goodness

Stephen and Saul

**Know what happened to Stephen and Saul.
Reflect on how God brings good out of evil.**

Stephen

As the number of disciples steadily increased, the apostles elected Stephen, a man of great faith, to help them. Stephen began to work miracles among the people.

Before long, he was arrested and brought before the High Council. In a powerful speech, he showed how the Old Testament prophecies about the Messiah had been fulfilled in Jesus.

He criticised the worship of the High Council and said, "You stubborn people, with your pagan hearts and pagan ears. You are always resisting the Holy Spirit, just as your ancestors used to do" (Acts 7: 51).

The members of the Council were furious and took his words as blasphemy. They dragged him outside the city and stoned him. Stephen was praying all the time and when the great stones began to strike him, he went on his knees and cried aloud as he died, "Lord, do not count this sin against them!"

Saul, a devout Jew approved of the stoning. But God had plans for him!

1. Stephen would have known that some of the Jewish leaders did not believe that Jesus was truly God.
   Was he right to speak openly about Jesus? Why? Why not?

2. In what ways was Stephen a true follower of Jesus?

3. Work in pairs.
   One of you is a Jewish reporter for the Jewish Chronicle and the other a Christian reporter for the Catholic Herald.
   Write a report on the stoning of Stephen.
   Think about:
   • what Stephen said about the Jews;
   • why they were so furious.
   Give your own opinion about what happened.

Saul

Saul was a Pharisee, a Jew who strictly followed the Jewish religious law.

His task was to make sure everyone observed it. As the Christians were not following the law, he believed it was his duty to use violence to persecute them. He went from house to house dragging the Christians out and putting them into prison (Acts 8:3).

He was on his way to Damascus determined to round up more Christians for prison when, suddenly, a bright light blazed down from heaven . It was so powerful he fell to the ground. A voice was speaking to him, **"Saul, Saul, why are you persecuting me?"**

Saul was very puzzled. "Who are you, Lord?" he asked.

"I am Jesus," the voice replied, **"and you are persecuting ME. Now get up and go into the city and you will be told what to do."**

The men with Saul were standing around looking astonished. They heard the voice, but they couldn't see anyone. Saul had to be led by the hand into the city of Damascus – he couldn't see at all. The bright light on the road had taken away his sight.

Ananias, a Christian living in Damascus, had a vision. He was told to go to the house where Saul was staying. He felt very nervous as he had heard that Saul was capturing Christians and putting them in prison – or worse! But he trusted in God. He went up to Saul, "Brother Saul", he said, "The Lord Jesus has sent me!"

As soon as Saul heard these words, he found he could see again. He was baptised immediately and was ready to talk about Jesus to other people. His name was changed to Paul. (Adapted from Acts 9:1-19).

Activities

1. a) What lesson did Jesus teach Saul on the road to Damascus?
   b) How does that lesson apply to us today?
   c) Give examples of how it should help us in school.
   d) Plan to live it fully for the next two days. Keep a diary so as to be able to share your experience.

2. What did Paul have to learn about Jesus in order to fulfil his mission as an apostle to the gentiles (those who were not Jewish)? Think about:
   • who Jesus is;
   • key points of his teaching;
   • the most important events in his life.

Paul and Silas

Paul in Damascus

Following his conversion, Saul's name was changed to Paul. He stayed with the disciples who were at Damascus for some days. He even went to the synagogue and spoke about Jesus. But this made some of the people in Damascus very cross. They didn't believe Jesus was the Son of God and they didn't want to hear about him at all. They certainly didn't want to hear about him from someone who had been capturing Christians until a few days ago!

After a few days, they began to make a plan to kill him, but Paul soon discovered the plot. He knew they were lying in wait, watching the gates of the city so they could catch him as he left.

However, Paul's new Christian friends had a plan. They found an enormous basket and waited until night time.
Paul climbed into the basket, crouched down inside and hid himself. Then his friends tied a strong rope to the handle of the basket and let Paul down out of the window, right down outside the wall of the city. He was safe – for now.

Pause to discuss

- What do you think Paul lost by becoming a Christian?
- What do you think he gained?
- What do you think he found most difficult?
- Who do you think gave him strength and courage?

Paul and Silas

Paul had a friend called Silas who went on journeys with him and helped him speak about Jesus to people who had never heard of him.

One day, Paul and Silas arrived at a town called Phillipi. As they always did when they arrived in a new town, Paul and Silas spoke about Jesus. They told the people of the town that Jesus is the Son of God, but truly human too. They explained that he performed miracles by healing the sick. They spoke about his teaching and how he died and rose again to save us all.

Activities

1. What did Paul and Silas do when they arrived in Philippi?

2. Work in pairs. Imagine you are Paul and Silas.
   - Plan a talk you will give to the people of Philippi.
   - Think about what you would say to make the people believe it was very important to hear the good news of Jesus.
   - Deliver your talk to the class.

Paul and Silas in prison

Some people were happy to hear this Good News, but others did not want to change their ways. Paul was able to help some of those who were sick, but even this did not please some of the men in the town. They took Paul and Silas to the magistrates.

"These men are disturbing our city!" they said. The magistrates agreed.

They ordered that Paul and Silas should be beaten and put in prison. The jailer was told to keep a close watch on them. So he followed his instructions, threw them into the inner prison and fastened their feet in the stocks.

Paul and Silas were glad to suffer for Jesus. They stayed awake. At midnight they were singing hymns when, suddenly there was a great earthquake. The floor of the prison shook, the doors were flung open and all the prisoners found themselves free.

The jailer rushed in, worried that his prisoners would escape and he would be punished.

"Don't worry," Paul called out to him. "We are still here!"
Paul and Silas told the jailer all about Jesus. Immediately he believed the Good News, and he and all his family were baptised. He took care of Paul and Silas until morning when the magistrates met. They decided to let Paul and Silas go free. (Adapted from Acts 16:23-35).

⏸ Pause to reflect
Sometimes we have to suffer. When this happens, it is an opportunity to have greater trust in God. We believe He will bring good out of evil and turn sadness into joy.

Activities

1. Paul and Silas were doing God's work, yet they were arrested.
   a) Why do you think this happened?
   b) How did they use this suffering to show their faith and trust in God?

2. Discuss. Who gained most from the experience of Paul and Silas?

3. Research: Find out about the challenges some Christians face today. Think about how we can help them.

The Cost of Discipleship

Know about Paul's missionary journeys.
Reflect on Paul's faith and courage.

A Disciple

To be a disciple means being a close friend of Jesus. Before returning to his Father in heaven, Jesus told his disciples that being a follower would not be easy. Here are some of the things he told them.

> "In the world you will have trouble, but be brave: I have conquered the world" (Jn. 16:33).

> "If they persecuted me, they will persecute you too…" (Jn. 15:20).

> "I will see you again and your hearts will be full of joy and that joy no one will take from you" (Jn. 16:22).

Paul's Mission

After Paul's conversion, he understood very clearly that he had a mission, a task to do. He was not only a disciple, he was an apostle. He had been sent out by Jesus to tell everyone the Good News of the resurrection, especially the 'gentiles' – those people who were not Jewish. He couldn't keep this news to himself and he spent the rest of his life travelling in order to tell the people about Jesus.

Paul visited places we still hear about today – Cyprus, Turkey and Rome – as well as lots of other places. Paul didn't travel alone. His first journey was with a friend called Barnabas.

At other times, he travelled with Silas, Luke and Timothy. Together they had many adventures.Near the end of his life, Paul wrote to some of his friends telling them of the difficult things that he had experienced as he brought the Good News to people.

"Five times I have been given the thirty-nine lashes … three times I have been beaten with sticks; once I was stoned; three times I have been shipwrecked, and once I have been in the open sea for a night and a day.

Continually travelling, I have been in danger from rivers, in danger from brigands, in danger from my own people and in danger from the gentiles, in danger in the towns and in danger in the open country, in danger at sea and in danger from people masquerading as brothers; I have worked with unsparing energy, for many nights without sleep; I have been hungry and thirsty, and often altogether without food or drink; I have been cold and lacked clothing" (2 Cor. 11:24-27).

The enemies of Paul could not understand how he had the courage to suffer such persecution with joy. Nothing would stop him spreading the Good News about the life, death and resurrection of Jesus.

Paul made many friends along the way and set up churches in their towns. When he was put in prison, he spent a lot of time writing to them, teaching them about Jesus. Many of these letters are now part of our Bible.

Activities

1. Jesus told his disciples what was likely to happen after he left them. (See page 85).
   a) What was challenging about his advice to them?
   b) What was good and hopeful about it?
   c) In what ways have his words come true?

2. a) How many times was Paul:
   - whipped?
   - beaten?
   - stoned?
   b) Why do you think:
   - he didn't give up?
   - he managed to survive all this persecution?

3. Study the picture of Paul being stoned on page 86.
   a) What do you think are the thoughts coming into his head?
   b) What do you think are the thoughts of those attacking him?
   c) If you had been there what would you have said to Paul?

The Teaching of the Apostles

Know some of the teaching of the Apostles.
Reflect on how this teaching helps us today.

God's Spirit at Work

The Holy Spirit had given the Apostles a new strength within them. This group of frightened fishermen were now filled with courage and self-confidence. They spoke openly about Jesus who had **died** and **risen from the dead**. Even their enemies could not understand how ordinary men could show such courage and accept difficulties, suffering and persecution with joy.

Teaching of the Apostles

No one could silence the Apostles. Even when they were warned to stop preaching they replied: "We cannot keep from speaking about what we have seen and heard" (Acts 4:20).

Frequently, Jesus is called the 'Christ' which means the Messiah. Jesus was the Messiah that the Jews were waiting for, but many did not recognise him.

Activities

1. Imagine you have been chosen to prepare to be an apostle.
   a) To begin, study some of the teaching of the Apostles.
   b) Select the teaching you want to make known.
   c) Plan:
      - **how** you will make it known, for example, on TV, YouTube;
      - **to whom** will you make it known;
      - whether you will work alone, in pairs or groups;
      - the resources you will need.

2. a) Quote the teaching which you are going to make known.
   b) Explain it in your own words.
   c) Give examples to show how you would put it into practice.

Some teaching of the Apostles

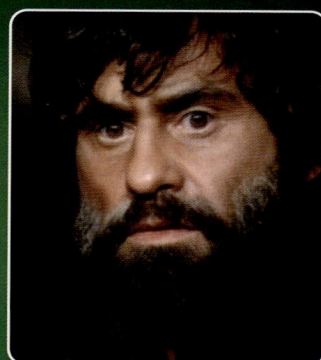

"My children,
our love is not to be just
words or mere talk, but
something real and
active."
            John (1Jn. 3:18).

"Love is always patient and kind;
it is never jealous; love is never
boastful or conceited; it is never
rude or selfish; it does not take
offence, and is not resentful."
            Paul (1Cor. 13:4-5).

"Bear with one another;
forgive each other as soon
as a quarrel begins. The
Lord has forgiven you; now
you must do the same."
            Paul (Col. 3:12-13).

"Love takes no pleasure in other
people's sins but delights in the
truth; it is always ready to
excuse, to trust, to hope, and
to endure whatever comes."
            Paul (1Cor. 13:6-7).

"The truth I have now come to realise is that God does not have
favourites, but anybody of any nationality who fears God and
does what is right is acceptable to him."
            Peter (Acts 10:34-35).

Key Points to Remember
List all the ways this teaching helps you.
Share with the class.

6. The Church

Understand that the Church is a family.
Be aware that we belong to the Church.

What is the Church?

As well as belonging to our own special family, we belong to the Church, the family of Christians, people like us who love Jesus and want to follow his teaching.

The Church began when the Holy Spirit descended on the apostles at Pentecost. They were the fishermen of Galilee who first met Jesus and were won over by his warm and strong personality. They responded to his loving and challenging invitation, **'Follow me, and I will make you become fishers of men'** (Mk. 1:17). They became the first members of the Church because they were his first followers. They heard all his teaching. They were witnesses of his miracles and his resurrection. So the Church, formed by the apostles, became a community of faith, hope and love.

- **Faith** – belief in God
- **Hope** – trust in God
- **Love** – love for God and one another

It is from Mary and the apostles that we receive the truth about Jesus. This truth is summed up in the Apostles' Creed. Here are some of the important statements which all Christians believe.

- God is our Father. He is totally powerful and eternal.
- God created heaven and earth.

- Jesus is the Son of God.
- Jesus was born, lived and died to save us from sin and death.
- Jesus rose from the dead and ascended into heaven.
- Jesus will come again.

A Parish

A parish is all the people in our Church family who live near each other. The parish family meet each week at Mass and at special times throughout the year to celebrate important occasions in our lives, for example, when we receive the Sacrament of Baptism.

This picture helps to give us an idea of what our parish, our local church is like. Study it carefully. Why do you think the parish church is in the middle of it?

Youth Club

Mothers & Toddlers Group

Mission Group

School

1. Discuss. What do you know about your parish?

2. a) In what way does your **school** help you to belong to the Church?
   Think about:
   - what you study;
   - what you learn from your studies;
   - what you do;
   - how you behave;
   - how you help others.
   b) What is the name of your school?
   Can you explain why that name is important?
   c) How does your school help you to be a true follower of Jesus?

3. Why do you think it is good to have a **Mothers and Toddlers** group?
   Give reasons.

4. a) Is a **Youth Group** important? Why? Why not?
   b) What do you think should happen in a church youth group? Why?

5. Design a webpage or newsletter to let people know about your parish.
   Include:
   - the name of your parish priest;
   - what he does;
   - what happens in the parish.

6. Imagine some inspectors are visiting the school.
   They know it is a Catholic school so they want to find out what Catholics believe.
   a) Work in pairs to make a list of questions they might ask.
   b) Share your questions with the class to make one long list.
   c) Play 'Hot-seating'. Take turns to be in the 'hot-seat' to answer some of the questions.

The Sacraments

Understand that the Church is 'good news' for people.
Be aware that this 'good news' is also for us.

The Journey of Life

Life is a *little bit* like a journey. It has a starting point and an end. Some time after our life journey begins we are able to walk without help.

Everyday, we need some nourishing food so that we are healthy and strong. Often there are times when we may fall or make wrong choices so we need help and guidance.

There are times when we have to make important choices about our future. Will we get married and have a family or choose another way of life? As we grow old and near the end of our journey, we may need extra help and support.

The 'Good News'

The Church is good news for us because at every stage in our Christian journey of life there is a special celebration to give us help and support. Each celebration is called a sacrament. A sacrament is a meeting between Jesus and the person who is receiving the sacrament.

When a person receives a sacrament they receive God's love, care and understanding – this is what we call God's grace.

Activities

1. a) What is the first sacrament a person is able to receive?
   b) What happens when the person receives this sacrament?

2. a) What is the sacrament we can receive when we make wrong choices and want to receive God's forgiveness?
   b) How often can we receive this sacrament?
   c) Why do you think it is 'good news'?

3. a) What is the sacrament in which we can receive Jesus?
   b) How does this sacrament help us?

Sacraments for Life

CONFIRMATION gives us the gifts of the Holy Spirit. We are given gifts which are not just for ourselves, but for us to use to help others. We are called by God to live more like Jesus and to share in the work of Jesus in our world.

MARRIAGE brings the blessing of Jesus. Jesus gives the married couple the help to love one another with God's love.

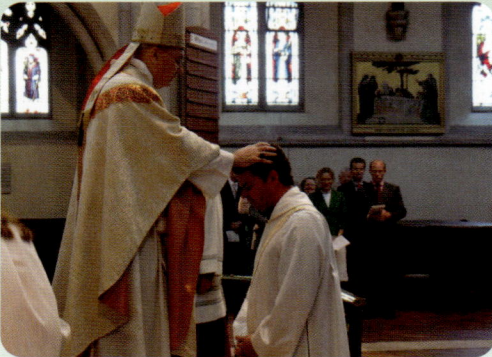

HOLY ORDERS is the sacrament when a man is ordained a priest. The Holy Spirit brings a special grace to help the priest act in the place of Jesus.

ANOINTING OF THE SICK gives strength, peace and courage to people suffering from a serious illness or from the weakness that comes from old age. This grace is a gift of the Holy Spirit to help us renew our faith and trust in God.

Activity

a) Work in pairs. Prepare two questions to ask about each of the seven sacraments: Baptism, Reconciliation, Eucharist, Confirmation, Marriage, Holy Orders, Anointing of the Sick.

b) Hot-seating. The class asks questions on the sacraments to the person in the hot-seat.

The Church's Year

The Liturgical Year

There are four seasons in the year – spring, summer, autumn and winter. The Church has seasons too. We call this the Liturgical Year. It celebrates events in the life of Jesus.

From the time of the Apostles, Christians gathered together on the first day of the week, the day of the resurrection of Jesus. We call Sunday the Lord's Day. Throughout the year, in between the Sundays, there are celebrations of various feasts of Jesus, Mary our Mother and the Saints.

The Liturgical Calendar

In the Church's year there are five seasons: Advent, Christmas, Lent, Easter and Ordinary Time. Each season has its own colour.

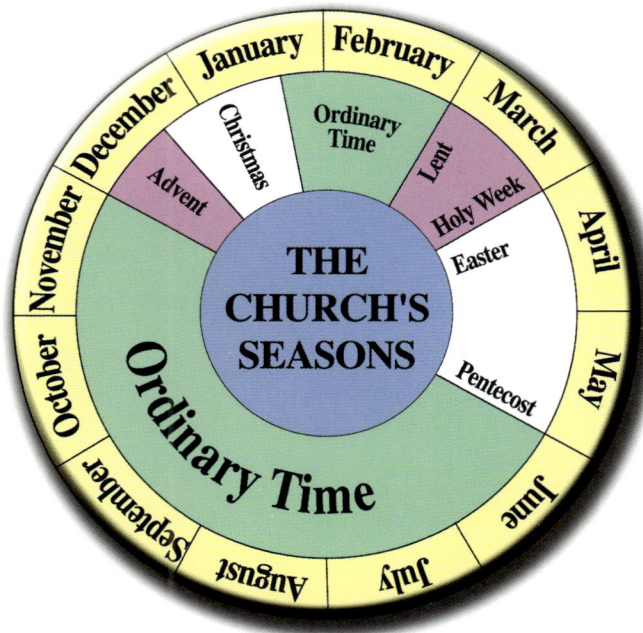

Activity

Which season do you think is the most important in the Church's year? Give reasons for your answer.

The Liturgical Colours

The priest usually wears vestments to match the colour of the season.

During **Advent** and **Lent** the priest wears purple. This is a sign of waiting, preparing and penance.

For Christmas and Easter the priest wears white and sometimes gold vestments. We celebrate joyful times in the life of Jesus.

Ordinary Time. For most of the year we are in Ordinary Time; we see the priest wearing green, the colour of hope, in our church. This is a time when we can try to grow closer to God by doing the ordinary things in our lives really well.

On certain occasions, the priest will wear red vestments although red does not have a whole season. Pentecost is a feast when red is worn because the colour reminds us of the fire which was the sign of the Holy Spirit. On the feast days of saints who were also martyrs, the priest wears red vestments.

We celebrate New Year on 1st January. This is when we might make New Year resolutions, start a new diary or hang up a new calendar. When you move into a new class, you are beginning a new year but this school year begins in September.

The Church's year begins on the First Sunday of Advent which is at the end of November or the beginning of December. You can see how the seasons of the Church's year follow each other and fit in with the months of the year in the seasons' wheel diagram on page 95.

1. a) Why is Sunday called the Lord's Day?
   b) What is the best way to celebrate it?
   c) How does the Church ask us to celebrate Sunday?

2. Here is a list of the five seasons of the Church. They are all jumbled up.
   a) Put them in the right order starting at the beginning of the Liturgical Year.
   b) Match them with one of the sentences in the box.
   c) Explain why each season is important.

   Lent

   Christmas

   Ordinary Time

   Advent

   Easter

   A time to celebrate the birth of Jesus

   A time to celebrate the presence of Jesus in our ordinary lives

   A time to celebrate that Jesus rose from the dead

   A time to prepare for Christmas

   A time to prepare for Easter

3. Research. Explain why the Church celebrates each of these feasts.

   Epiphany   The Annunciation   Pentecost Sunday

4. Why do you think the Church begins a New Year with the season of Advent?

   (Clue: what comes after Advent, how are these seasons linked?)

5. Why is red a good colour for Pentecost and feast days of saints who became martyrs?

The Communion of Saints

What is the Communion of Saints?

In the Apostles' Creed there is a phrase the '**communion of saints**'. This is a very important phrase because it is talking about the whole Church. The Communion of Saints means all the people in the Church.

There are a lot more people in the Church than those who are still living here on earth. The Communion of Saints also includes many people who belonged to the Church who have now died and gone to heaven and those who have died and are waiting to go to heaven. We belong to a very big community.

Belonging to a community means we try to help each other. The saints in heaven are always in the presence of God and they are happy to help us as we try to live our lives in the way God asks. We can speak to the saints in our prayers and ask them to pray for us.

Activities

1. Study this picture carefully.
   a) How do you think it illustrates the Communion of Saints?

2. a) Make your own illustration of the Communion of Saints.
   b) Write an explanation for it.

The Holy Souls

Some people who have died are not yet ready for heaven, but they are still part of the Communion of Saints. God is very loving and He allows them to wait until they are ready to meet Him. These people are the Holy Souls and we can help them by our prayers and by offering small sacrifices for them.

Prayers for the Holy Souls:

May their souls,
and the souls of all the faithful departed
through the mercy of God
rest in peace. Amen

Eternal rest grant to them O Lord
and let perpetual light shine upon them.
May they rest in peace. Amen

A Sacrifice

Here is the way Robert made a small sacrifice for the Holy Souls:

Robert was in the lunch time queue at school. He waited patiently and didn't push. This meant some other children got in before him. When he came to the front, there was none of his favourite pizza left. Robert took some salad instead, which he didn't really like. As he ate it, he thought of his grandmother who had died. He spoke to God in his head.

"If Grandma is waiting with the Holy Souls, please use this small sacrifice to help her be with you in heaven. If she's already in heaven, please use it for someone who needs it."

Activities

1. Work in pairs. Suggest ways in which we can help the Holy Souls on their feast day, 2nd November.

2. a) Learn the prayers for the Holy Souls.
   b) When you know them, test each other.

The Mission of the Church

The Mission of Jesus

Before returning to his Father, Jesus passed his mission on to his disciples and through them to the Church. He said,

Go therefore and make disciples of all nations

"Go therefore and make disciples of all nations, baptising them in the name of the Father and of the Son and of the Holy Spirit, teaching them to observe all that I have commanded you; and lo, I am with you always, until the end of time" (Mt. 28: 19-20).

Activity

Read again the mission that Jesus gave to his disciples.
a) What was the first thing the disciples had to do?
b) What is the second thing they had to do?
c) What promise did Jesus make to them?

The Church has spread throughout the world

Since the time of Jesus, the apostles and those who lived after them, have tried to do what Jesus said. They have travelled all over the world to bring the Good News of Jesus' resurrection to everyone. They want everyone to be members of the family of Jesus, the Church. Now there are many, many people all over the world who have heard about Jesus. However, missionaries are still needed today even in our own country.

Blessed John Paul II, the Missionary Pope

Pope John Paul was a true missionary. He could speak ten languages, a gift which helped him when he visited over one hundred and forty countries. These visits included countries where there were few Christians such as China, Vietnam, Russia, Iraq, Iran and Algeria. In some of these countries, Christians are sometimes persecuted for their faith.

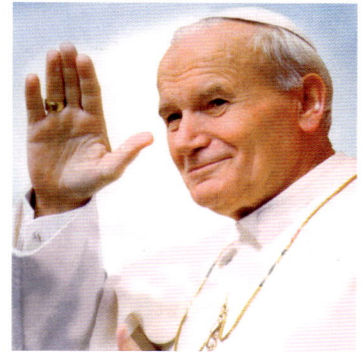

Pope John Paul was like a loving father to all the people. Everywhere he went, thousands and thousands flocked to hear him speak about Jesus.

Young people loved him. Almost every year, he called them together from all over the world for 'World Youth Days'.

"As the Father sent me, so am I sending you"
Jn 20: 21

The Pope's message to all young people is, that they must be like the first Christians and radiate enthusiasm and courage for the mission of Jesus in their own countries.

In his old age, Pope John Paul became very ill, but he still visited as many people and places as possible. He was still a missionary for Jesus. Just as the Holy Saturday vigil for Easter was beginning in April 2005, John Paul died peacefully.

Activities

1. Work in small groups.
   a) What do you think Pope John Paul II meant by asking young people to 'radiate enthusiasm and courage for the mission of Jesus'?
   b) Suggest ways you could do it.

2. Research in pairs. Find out which countries have hosted a World Youth Day. Choose one and make a Power Point presentation about it to show to the class.

Blessed Mother Teresa of Calcutta

Mother Teresa was born in Albania, 26th August, 1910. When she was eight years old, her father died and when she was eighteen, she entered the convent of the Sisters of Loreto in Ireland.

Later, she was sent to India where she taught students from wealthy families in St. Mary's High School in Calcutta. During this time, she felt Jesus was calling her to serve him in the poorest of the poor.

Mother Teresa received permission to leave the convent and move into a small house in the slums. At first, it was very difficult because she had to beg for money to help the hungry, the homeless, the lepers and all those who felt unwanted and unloved.

Before long, she was joined by other women who wanted to help and they became known as the Missionaries of Charity.

When people saw the great work that Mother Teresa and her companions were doing, they wanted to donate money.
Soon, centres were opened for the sick, the homeless, the unwanted and the unloved, not only in India but all over the world.

Mother Teresa believed that "to show great love for God and our neighbour, we don't need to do great things. It is how much love we put in the doing that makes our offering something beautiful for God". Her message to everyone who wanted to help was, "We can do no great things, only small things with great love".

Mother Teresa was able to love everyone because it was Jesus living in her, who gave her the strength and courage to do so.

When asked who Jesus was for her, Mother Teresa said,

> **"Jesus is my God,**
> **Jesus is my Spouse,**
> **Jesus is my Life,**
> **Jesus is my only Love,**
> **Jesus is my All in All;**
> **Jesus is my Everything."**

Mother Teresa died in 1997 and was beatified in 2003. Her beatification means that the Church recognised that she was a person who had led a very holy life and was on the way to being canonised a saint.

Activities

1. a) What did Mother Teresa do that we could do every day and it doesn't cost money?
   b) Give an example of how you could do it.

2. Any gift we give to God, He will transform into something beautiful. Mother Teresa made a gift of her life to God. In what ways did God transform this gift?
   (Clue: Think about what she was able to do).

3. Discuss.
   Mother Teresa gave up teaching in a school to help the homeless, the sick and the unloved.
   - Why do you think she did this?
   - Do you think she made the right decision? Give reasons.
   - Why might some people not agree with you?

4. Work in pairs.
   Imagine that both of you are preparing to go as missionaries to a country where people have never heard about God.
   a) Choose to go as a teacher, a doctor, a nurse, a priest or a nun. Give reasons for your choice.
   b) Use bullet points to plan what you would like to do when you get there.
   c) Explain why you would want to do these things.

Mary, Mother of the Church

What do we know about Mary?

The Annunciation

The angel Gabriel appeared to Mary and called her the highly-favoured one, full of grace. The angel told her that God had chosen her to have a very important part in His plan for all of us.

Mary was amazed that God was asking her to be the mother of the Messiah, the Saviour of the world. "But how can this happen?' she asked.

The angel explained that the Holy Spirit would come down upon her and she would be overshadowed by the power of the Father. There would be a miracle within her so that she would be the Mother of God's own Son, Jesus. Mary offered her life to God, 'Let it be done to me as God wants'.

Pause to reflect

All Mary wants is what God wants for her.

The Visitation

The angel told Mary that her cousin Elizabeth was also going to have a baby even though she was a very old lady. Mary knew that Elizabeth would need help, so she set out on a long journey to visit her.

The minute they met, Elizabeth knew that something very special had happened to Mary because the baby in her womb leapt for joy. They were both so happy. Mary sang her 'Magnificat'; a song of praise about the wonderful things God does.

The Magnificat

The people who are hungry for God's Word:
they will be filled with good things.
The rich who are full of themselves:
they will be sent away empty.
The mighty who think they are powerful and
self-sufficient: they will be humbled.
The humble people, those with an open-heart
seeking God: they will be exalted.

Pause to discuss

Can you think of an example of
- a person who is hungry for God?
- some people who are rich and full of themselves?
- the powerful and self-sufficient?
- the humble person with an open-heart for God?

Loss and Finding of Jesus in the Temple

Mary and Joseph had three worrying days looking for Jesus. When they found him, Mary said, 'Son, why have you done this to us? Your father and I have been looking for you'. He replied, 'Did you not know that I must be doing the things that belong to my Father?'

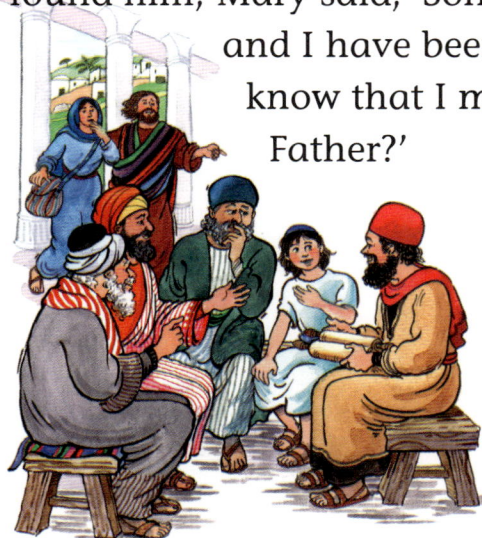

Mary and Joseph did not understand what Jesus meant. But Mary knew that God was teaching her something. She wanted only what God wanted, even though at the time, she did not understand God's plan (Lk. 2:41-52).

Pause to reflect

Mary is teaching us that God is in charge. As He looked after Mary and Joseph, God is looking after us. However, that does not mean that we will always understand what is happening.
We must learn to continually trust God and let God guide our lives.

Wedding Feast at Cana

Mary was with Jesus at the wedding feast. During the feast she noticed that the wine was all gone. She knew that the newly married couple would feel very embarrassed about it. She told Jesus what had happened. He gave the strange reply, "My hour has not yet come". Mary continued to trust that Jesus would help. She told the servants, "Do whatever he tells you".

Activity

a) Use your Bible.
   Read Jn. 2:1-11.
b) What did Jesus say to the servants?
c) What happened next?

The **Miracle at Cana** shows us that when we need help, if we make our request to Mary, she will ask her son, Jesus, to help us.

The Crucifixion

When Jesus was being crucified, Mary and John stayed with him all the time. Just before he died, Jesus told John that Mary was now his mother (Jn. 19:25-27).

In this way, Jesus was asking Mary to look after all of us. Mary has become the **mother of all the members of the Church**. She is the mother of the family of the Church. Mary is our spiritual mother and will always help us when we turn to her.

Make your own 'Key Points to Remember'.

Devotion to Mary in the Church

In many countries all over the world there are shrines to Our Lady. Lourdes is one of the most popular as thousands of sick people go there every year to ask Mary to help them.

Our Lady of Lourdes

In 1858, a young girl called Bernadette lived in the small village of Lourdes in France. Her parents were very poor people and Bernadette was often ill. One day, she was near a river gathering fire wood. Suddenly, she looked up and saw a beautiful lady. The lady spoke to her and asked her to pray, to do penance and to have a chapel built there.

To start with, no-one would believe Bernadette, but the lady appeared to her many times. One time, she told Bernadette to dig in the mud, and when she did so, a stream of clear water appeared. Soon people began to bathe in the spring and many were healed. A chapel was built and many thousands of people still go to Lourdes every year, to pray and to bathe in the water.

Bernadette has been canonised, that means that the Church believes she is a saint.

The feast of Our Lady of Lourdes is celebrated on 11 February and St. Bernadette on16 April.

Activities

1. Research. Find out about other places of pilgrimage to Our Lady. For example,
   - Fatima
   - Guadalupe
   - Czestochowa
   - Knock

2. The Church celebrates many feast days of Our Lady.
   Your teacher will give you a list of some of them.
   Use your ICT skills to research one.
   Make a Big Book on Mary for your class.

Glossary

Alms — Money given to the poor

Ancestors — The members of your family from whom you are descended

Angel — A messenger from God

Annunciation — When the Angel Gabriel announced to Our Lady that she would be the Mother of God's Son.

Anoint — Putting oil on a person's head to show they have been chosen by God

Apostle — The twelve closest followers of Jesus whose mission was to begin the Church

Ascension — When Jesus went back up to heaven

Beatification — A special ceremony to declare that the Church believes someone has led a very holy life

Bishop — A priest who is chosen to be leader of a diocese

Blessings — Good things that come from God

Brigand — A robber

Canonisation — This is when the Church is sure a person is in heaven and adds them to the list of saints

Charity — Love for God and one another

Chosen one — The person God promised would save His people

Conceived — The moment when a life begins

Conscience — It is the feeling inside me telling me what is right and what is wrong

Convent — The place where people who have dedicated their whole lives to God live together.

Covenant — A very serious promise between two people, or between God and people

Creation — All that God creates in the universe, the world, animals, plants and people

Creed	From the Latin word credo which means 'I believe'. It is an important list of the things Christians believe
Descendants	Those in your family who come after you, your children, grandchildren and their children
Devout	A devout person follows their religion carefully
Diocese	An area with lots of parishes with a bishop to look after them
Disciples	The people who follow and listen to Jesus
Engaged	When two people promise that they will marry each other
Epiphany	The three wise men seeing the baby Jesus
Eternal life	A life with God that never ends
Eucharist	Another name for the Mass
Faith	Belief in God
False Gods	Things that take the place of God in our lives, like possessions
Favour	God's kindness and blessing
Foster father	A man who looks after a child in place of his real father
Frankincense	A spice burned to make a sweet smell
Garden of Gethsemane	A Garden outside Jerusalem also known as the Mount of Olives where Jesus liked to pray
Gentiles	People who are not Jewish
Glory	The honour and praise that God deserves
Gold	A precious metal which is a suitable gift for a King
Good News	The meaning of the word Gospel
Grace	A help or gift which comes from God
Handmaid	A servant, ready to do whatever God wants
Holy Souls	The people who have died and are preparing to meet God in heaven
Humble	A humble person does not boast about how important or clever they are, or about the things they have or do.

Incarnation	When the Son of God became man
Incense	A spice which is burned to make a sweet smell
Jewish religion	The religion which began with Abraham and to which Jesus belonged
Judas	The disciple who betrayed Jesus
Lamb of God	A name given to Jesus because he was sacrificed for our sins
Last Supper	Jesus' last Passover meal with his disciples when he gave them the Sacrament of Eucharist for the first time
Latin	The language spoken by the Romans and still the official language of the Catholic Church
Lent	The forty days before Easter when we prepare for the death and resurrection of Jesus
Lepers	People suffering from the dreadful disease called leprosy, or Hansen's Disease
Locust	An insect
Magnificat	The song of praise Mary sang to God at Elizabeth's house (Luke 1:46-55)
Martyr	Somebody who is a witness to Jesus and then dies or suffers for what they believe
Maundy Thursday	Another name for Holy Thursday, the Thursday in Holy Week.
Mercy	Kindness and forgiveness
Messiah	The person who God promised would save His people
Mission	The task of teaching or preaching the Word of God
Missionary	A person who spreads the Word of God by what they say and do
Myrrh	A spice used to put on the bodies of people who have died
Nineveh	A great city in the ancient world, capital of the Assyrian Empire
Pagan	Someone who did not believe in the one true God
Passover meal	The special meal that Jews have to remember their escape from Egypt

Pentecost	An important Jewish feast day and the day when the Holy Spirit came down on the apostles
Perpetual	Something that is always there
Philistines	A warlike people who lived near Israel
Plague	Something bad which affects many people
Pope	The person who takes the place of St. Peter as leader of the Church on earth
Prophets	Someone who proclaims God's messages and speaks by divine inspiration
Religion	Believing in God and trying to live as He asks us
Repent	To be sorry for your sins
Resurrection	When Jesus rose from the dead on Easter Sunday
Roman governor	The person sent by the Roman Emperor to rule a part of the empire
Sacrifice	To give something precious to God
Salvation	To be saved by God from sin and death so we can share His life
Scrolls	Rolls of paper or parchment where the Word of God was written
Shrine	A holy place where people go to pray
Swaddling clothes	Strips of cloth used to wrap new babies in
Unleavened bread	A flat bread made with no yeast
Visitation	The time when Mary went to see her cousin Elizabeth
Wilderness	A place where no-one lives
Womb	The place inside a mother where her baby grows
Worship	To adore, respect, praise
Writing tablet	A wax tablet used in Roman times instead of writing paper

Acknowledgments

Second and revised edition: May 2013

Nihil obstat: Father Anton Cowan – Censor.

Imprimatur: The Most Rev. Vincent Nichols PhL, MA, Med, STL,
Archbishop of Westminster.
Holy Thursday, 28 March 2013

The *Nihil obstat* and *Imprimatur* are a declaration that the books and contents of the CD ROM are free from doctrinal or moral error. It is not implied that those who have granted the *Nihil obstat* and the *Imprimatur* agree with the contents, opinions or statements expressed.

Theological Advisor: Fr Bryan Lobo SJ
Picture Research: Sr Marcellina Cooney CP & Ian Curtis

© 2013 Sr Marcellina Cooney CP – Design & Text
© 2013 Ian Curtis, First Sight Graphics, firstsightgraphics.com – Design, Compilation & Format

Illustrations: © Jenny Williams; © Philip Hood, Arena Illustrations; © Bob Farley, Graham-Cameron Illustrations; © Peter Dennis

Acknowledgements
Considerable thanks are due to the head teachers of the following schools for making it possible for their teachers to attend Editorial Meetings: St. Vincent's Primary, Barnet NW7; St. Vincent's Primary, Bromley SE9; Holy Ghost Primary, Wandsworth SW12; St. Joseph's Primary, Wandsworth SW15; Ursuline Preparatory School, Brentwood CM13.

Permission credits
Cover illustration © Philip Hood/Arena Illustrations; page 22 photo © Marcellina Cooney CP; page 27 © Prophecy of John's Birth, © Heinemann/ AKG Images; page 30 Annunciation to Mary, © Fra Angelico/AKG Images; page 34 Adoration of the Shepherds, © Maella, Mariano Salvador de (1739-1819) Rafael Valls Gallery, London; page 36 Adoration of the Kings, © Dolci, Carlo (1616-1686) National Gallery; pages 37, 68, 69, 89 © ITV Global Entertainment; 38, 70, 71 stained glass windows from St. Luke's Catholic Church, Dunmury, Belfast BT17 Diocese of Down & Connor, photos used with permission from Rev Darach Mac Giolla Catháin; page 39 stained glass window St. Matthias Catholic Church, Belfast BT11 and used with permission of Fr. Brendan Beagan PP © CWS Design, 9 Ferguson Drive, Lisburn BT28 2EX; page 46 Baptism of Jesus by John the Baptist, © English School 19th Century Bridgeman Art Library; page 87 stained glass window from St Aloysius Catholic Church, Phoenix Road, London NW1 taken by Marcellina Cooney CP with permission of Rev James McNicholas PP; page 82 Saul flees Damascus, G. De Sanctis (1829-1911) © Basilica Papale di San Paolo fuori le Mura; page 86 Stoning of Paul in Lystra, C. Mariani (1826-1901) © Basilica Papale di San Paolo fuori le Mura; page 94 photo of Confirmation © Marcellina Cooney CP; page 94 photo of Marriage © Diana Pereira; photo of Ordination © Society of Jesus, UK; page 98 by Elizabeth Wang © Radiant Light; page 102 Mother Teresa in Calcutta © Kakpoor Baldev, Sygma/CORBIS; © Lisa S./Shutterstock.com; © VikaSuh/Shutterstock.com; © AlexSmith/Shutterstock.com; © Attitude/Shutterstock.com; © Oleksiy Mark/Shutterstock.com; © argus/Shutterstock.com; © Artem Loskutnikov/Shutterstock.com; © Vphoto/Shutterstock.com; © HunThomas/Shutterstock.com; © artproem/Shutterstock.com; © SergiyN/Shutterstock.com; © andreiuc88/Shutterstock.com; © file404/Shutterstock.com; © gkuna/Shutterstock.com; © Monkey Business Images/Shutterstock.com; © David M. Schrader/Shutterstock.com; © Norph/Shutterstock.com; © somkcr/Shutterstock.com; © Click Bestsellers/Shutterstock.com; © Karma Shuford/Shutterstock.com; © YRoma/Shutterstock.com; © photoslb com/Shutterstock.com; © venimo/Shutterstock.com; © turtleteeth/Shutterstock.com; © Hollygraphic/Shutterstock.com; © Hluboki Dzianis/Shutterstock.com; © Triff/Shutterstock.com; © Sergej Razvodovskij/Shutterstock.com; © Dominik Hladik/Shutterstock.com; © Seamartini Graphics/Shutterstock.com; © Vasaleks/Shutterstock.com.

Every effort has been made to contact copyright holders. Any omissions will be rectified in subsequent printings if notice is given to the Teachers' Enterprise in Religious Education Co. Ltd, 40 Duncan Terrace, London N1 8AL

Printed in the UK by Geerings Print Ltd, www.geeringsprint.co.uk